WHAT C

"As soon as you trust yourself,
you will know how to live."

Johann Wolfgang von Goethe

"Elaine Grohman writes from the heart about matters that are
vital to all of us. It is remarkable how many people say she has
changed and improved their lives. Her work in energy healing
is powerful and provocative, as is this book."

Jeffrey Zaslow, co-author of the New York Times best seller,
The Last Lecture

"Fascinating and Enlightening! If you're holding this book,
there's a reason for it. Read on!"

Jennifer Skiff
Author - *God Stories: Inspiring Encounters with the Divine*

"A book that is not only timely in today's unpredictable world,
but required reading for anyone interested in understanding the
human spirit and condition more deeply. Elaine Grohman pulls
back the veil to show we are not alone, and how connected we
really are to the abundant and powerful healing energy around
us. Her prose is clear and compelling, and she writes with the
force of her own truth, personal and vulnerable. 'Angels' is
also a subtle challenge to those who believe there is nothing
after death, and gives hope to those suffering from all the very
human ills that life contains."

Andrew Heyman, M.D., M.H.S.A.
Program in Integrative Medicine
Department of Family Medicine
University of Michigan

"Elaine is a gifted healer, well grounded in this world, while having access to realms far beyond."

Leonard D. Wright, M.D.
Medical Director - Spectrum Hospice, Grand Rapids, MI

"Elaine Grohman has energy and insight to share with anyone who has an open heart and open mind. I have been impressed with her ability to reach patients, medical students, and health professionals alike!"

Sara L. Warber, M.D.
Co-Director, University of Michigan Integrative Medicine
Associate Professor, University of Michigan
Department of Family Medicine

"I have known Elaine Grohman over the years and observed her art - visual, human and spiritual - at work. She is a truly gifted and exceptional individual. In a very special way, her work gently reminds us that we are spirits existing, for the time being, in a human world.

Among health care providers, I have seen some of the most skeptical biomedically-oriented providers become profoundly moved and elevated in their thinking, returning to their professional lives determined to practice in a more enlightened way. The lives she touches are changed, and forever more spiritually connected."

Robert Jarski, Ph.D.
Professor, School of Health Sciences and
The Oakland University-William Beaumont School of Medicine
Director, Complementary Medicine & Wellness
Certificate Program
Oakland University - Rochester, Michigan

"*Elaine Grohman combines her intuitive wisdom along with energy healing, making for a powerful experience. Over the years I have worked with Elaine, having had the honor of receiving healing treatments. She not only assists in clearing and balancing one's energy, but offers meaningful information and connection to the spiritual guides and guidance available to us all. Elaine works from a place of integrity, serving as an earth angel and contributing her part to the raising of the consciousness and healing of this planet.*"

Rebecca Rosen - Medium and author of *Spirited*, to be released in February 2010
Denver, Colorado
www.rebeccarosen.com

"*Angels take many forms and I have found my own personal angel/healer in Elaine. Her compassion, integrity and open heart allow you to feel instantly connected and at ease. As if you have come into the presence of someone indeed special and unique - a gift from God .*

I just know your book will touch the lives of so many people, allowing the healing balm of words to sink into their souls so they can move forward with hope and appreciation in the knowledge that we all have gifts and experiences that sometimes we take for granted, not realizing they are indeed a message or a visitation from Angels."

Georgina Walker, Psychic Intuitive
Author of *Dearly Departed* and *Amazing Encounters*
Sydney, Australia

"Elaine Grohman is spiritually interconnected with the universal nature of those things that cultivate and strengthen the sacred grace of our humanness. For me, personally, she is also an extraordinary healing force. Her dedicated compassion released my fears, affirmed my strengths and resisted the forces of death at a time when I needed to reclaim my life from Leukemia. As an inspirational facilitator of therapeutic balancing and personal transformation her book is to be treasured as a gift from a loving heart." (You will find Robert's story in Chapter 10)

Robert Piepenburg - Artist, Teacher, and author of
The Spirit of Ceramic Design: Cultivating Creativity With Clay, Raku Pottery, The Spirit of Clay: A Classic Guide to Ceramics, and *Treasures of the Creative Spirit*

DEDICATION

I thank God for giving me the wisdom to listen to my heart,
to learn from the joy and sadness in life
and to begin to understand that the lesson is one of Love.

To my father, Jack Hughes, and my stepmother, Jane Wolford Hughes,
and to my wonderful siblings,
Judy, Chris, Dianne, John, Brian, Michael, Maureen, Paul, Therese,
Diane, Maureen, Mike, Jim, John and Joe.
To my sisters and brothers-in-law, Bill, Jack, Claire, Lisa, Dave, Joanne,
Mark, Cathy, Maureen, Jeff, Bob, and Sandy.
You have all helped me to see the incredible value of love
in all its many disguises.

To my husband and children, Richard, Elaine and Brian,
we have taught each other many lessons
as we have walked this life together.
Always know that you are my dearest treasures.

To my son-in-law, Marvin, and my future daughter-in-law, Ronya,
we are blessed to have you join our family.

To my precious grandchildren, Maria and Conner,
may your eyes and hearts always be open
to the Love that is all around you.

To my dear and treasured friends, you bring joy into my life.

And of course, to the Angels, for their ever present
Love, Trust and Compassion for the Human Race.

But especially, to my mother,
Elaine Prevost Hughes,
whose examples of love showed us how to love,
and how loved we were.
For that I will forever be grateful.

The author of this book does not dispense medical advice or prescribe the use of any technique as a form of treatment for physical, emotional or medical problems. One should seek the advice of their physician or health care provider. The intent of the author is to offer information of a general nature to help the reader in their quest for self-aware-ness and well-being. In the event that you use any of the information provided in this book for yourself, which is your right, the author and/or the publisher assume no respon-sibility for your actions.

Library of Congress Control Number: 2009909475
Grohman, Elaine M.

ISBN # 978-0-9820268-1-6
Printed in the United States of America

Grohman, Elaine M.
The angels and me : experiences of receiving and sharing
divine communications / Elaine M. Grohman. -- Columbus, Ohio :
Seraph Books, L.L.C., 2009.
p. ; cm.
ISBN: 978-0-9820268-1-6
1. Energy medicine. 2. Integrative medicine. 3. Alternative
medicine. 4. Self-care, Health. 5. Angels. 6. Spirituality. 7. Spiritual
healing. 8. Intuition. 9. Visions. 10. Prophecies. I. Title.
II. Experiences of receiving and sharing divine communications.
BT966.3 .G76 2009 2009909475
235.3--dc22 0911

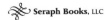 Seraph Books, LLC

THE Angels AND ME

EXPERIENCES OF RECEIVING AND SHARING DIVINE COMMUNICATIONS

Mona
Trust the goodness
within you !
Elaine M. Grohman ♡

ELAINE M. GROHMAN

TABLE OF CONTENTS

	What Others Have to Say	
	Dedication	
	Introduction	1
Chapter 1	Answering an Unanswerable Prayer	8
Chapter 2	Watching an Angel	16
Chapter 3	My Wounding	20
Chapter 4	A Moment to Remember	26
Chapter 5	This Is What It Is	30
Chapter 6	Forgiveness	34
Chapter 7	Build a Quiet Mind	38
Chapter 8	Surrounded by Grace	40
Chapter 9	Listening	49
Chapter 10	Getting the Message	52
Chapter 11	The Breath of an Angel	62
Chapter 12	Going Beyond Our Boundaries	70
Chapter 13	The Seen and the Unseen	77
Chapter 14	The Releasement	82
Chapter 15	Learning to Trust	90
Chapter 16	A Young Man's Wounds in an Old Man's Body	94
Chapter 17	Sweet Andrea	98
Chapter 18	The Man in the Bathroom	101
Chapter 19	Lighten Up	104
Chapter 20	Remembering Why	111
Chapter 21	It's All About Love	114
Chapter 22	A Message to Her Mother	116
Chapter 23	Healing a Wounded Heart	120

Chapter 24	Moving Through Space and Time	126
Chapter 25	The Season of Goodness	132
Chapter 26	Be the Gift	137
Chapter 27	The Power of a Loving Heart	140
Chapter 28	The Beautiful Ribbons of Love	148
Chapter 29	Transforming Sorrow into Joy	152
Chapter 30	Love ….the Elixir of Life	158
Chapter 31	Be Grateful	162
Chapter 32	Bring Goodness to Where You Stand	165
Chapter 33	Divine + Force = Amazing	170
Chapter 34	A Little Peanut in the Big Apple	177
Chapter 35	The Medicine Walk	188
Chapter 36	The Voice of Your Holy Selves	194
Chapter 37	The Impact of a Transgression	200
Chapter 38	The Surest Guide	203
Chapter 39	Tell Daddy for Me	207
Chapter 40	The Opened Door	213
Chapter 41	Francesca - The Miracle Baby	218
Chapter 42	Touching the Web of Life	222
Chapter 43	Until You Know	228
Chapter 44	The Nail	231
Chapter 45	Close the Door of Anger	234
Chapter 46	Expect a Miracle	238
	Acknowledgments	241
	References	243
	About the Author	245

INTRODUCTION

"Begin at the beginning,
it is the best place to start."

Elaine M. Grohman

The Angels are among us. We have heard that so many times. Yet, how many of us actually believe it is true? There are Divine Beings whose purpose is to help us, to be our truest friends, to guide us, even though we often do not listen, and to always love us, even more than we could possibly love ourselves. Such are the gifts that the Angelic Beings bring to our lives, if we are wise enough to pay attention, and if we are humble enough to know that there is so very little that we truly know.

Never in a million years would I have thought that I would work with the Angels. And, not only work with them, but also be amazed at the ways that they use circumstances and events to bring messages of love to us all. I thought I knew about Angels; after all, I was raised in a Catholic family and images of Angels were everywhere. I had seen them painted on the walls of the church, magnificently gleaming from stained glass windows, breathless as they were embodied in stone sculptures, memorized in prayers, and hanging from Christmas trees. They could be seen everywhere, if only one would look.

But what if you could actually hear them, sense them, and communicate with them? What would happen to one's perception of

1

life and living? Would you comprehend that you are never fully alone, even in your darkest hours? What if all of this were true, and that all it took was one experience to change your whole perception of everything?

I have experienced many of those moments, and it is here, in the pages of this book, that I would like to share with you some of the many ways that Angels have shared their wisdom, shared their love and even protected me from harm. All I needed to do was listen, believe, trust, and know that they are always near and always have our best interest at heart.

This book is meant to give you a glimpse into that which seems impossible, but is all together true, perhaps truer than anything else that you have experienced in this world. Angels, by definition, are Messengers. The word Angel, which ends in "el," indicates a messenger. The vast majority of Angels that most people are familiar with have names that end in "el." For example, the Archangels Michael, Gabriel, Raphael, and Uriel are just some of the many names that you may have heard. However, Angels do not really care that you know their names; and in reality, many are known as the "Unknowable Ones." Yet, they will guide us and bring great wisdom and understanding to our human condition, if we only invite them in.

Long before I began to do Angel Readings, and then Audience Angel Readings, I was being comforted and gently guided by my Angel friends. Through times of deep sorrow and confusion, the Angels helped me to see that all is not as it seems. Through the difficulty of profound loss we can begin to eventually see that there is a Light at the end of the tunnel and indeed that we are truly standing at all times within the Light, but we often have our eyes squeezed shut, believing that the darkness that we see with our eyes closed is the darkness that surrounds us. There is no darkness outside of the human heart. We create and strengthen that darkness when we refuse to open up. Even the tiniest flame diminishes the darkness, and the bogeyman of our imagination is brought to the light of day.

Many times we have heard stories of people being whisked out of harm's way, or being comforted by a stranger, only to find that the stranger had vanished into thin air. We may even choose to think that these stories are myths. Yet, within the confines of each myth lies a vision of truth that gives us a glimpse into ourselves and of which we are a part, the All That Is.

There are more stories than I could possibly put into one book because the stories are a lifetime of awakenings. Some of what I share in these pages are experiences that I have had while working as an Energy Healer, some as an Educator, some as an Angel Reader and some are "pearls of wisdom" shared with me as I prepared for an Audience Angel Reading.

My life changed drastically one precious day, and all that I knew deep within me was awakened. Shortly thereafter I began to learn about Energy Medicine, which served to further open my gifts of intuition and confirmed many deep thoughts and experiences that I held silently within. All of my life, from the time I was a child, I knew that Angels were with me. I could feel them, I could hear them, and in times of deep sadness I felt that my ever-present friends, the Angels, were the only ones who could help me heal my own heart.

After several years of doing individual readings, I was "told" that it was time to work with larger groups of people. Nervously I complied, worrying that I would not be able to help many people at the same time. "Trust Us" was the constant feeling. The truth is, it wasn't Them that I didn't trust, it was my own limitations that made me concerned. I shouldn't have worried.

As a way of quieting my apprehension of doing Audience Readings, the Angels suggested that I listen and write "Their Message" which I would read at the beginning of each group event. Their messages are intended to set the tone for the evening. Each and every time it has been exactly what needed to be said to the group that night. So I would sit at my computer, internally ask for their message, and within moments my fingers would fly across the keys of my laptop and before I knew it the message was complete. I would read it for the first time myself once my fingers stopped moving. It didn't seem to matter if I had hours before the reading or if I found that I had minutes to spare before leaving to drive to the location of the event. Minutes are all it takes to get the message across.

So each and every time I have done an Audience Reading, I read their message that sets the tone for the evening. The messages are simple yet powerful, and I will share many of those messages with you on the pages of this book.

I will also share with you many of my personal communications from the Angels. Sometimes the messages were only for me and other times the messages were for the people with me. Each time, however, I was privileged to become more fully aware of the Love that surrounds us all, even in the depths of our grief.

I am in no way different then anyone else: I was born; I have had laughter and tears, frustrations and triumphs, injuries and healing, and surely someday I will die. We are all meant to experience these things; but when the trials of life become a burden to our hearts, it is then that we believe that we are alone, or worse, that we don't matter. The Angels want us to know that each and every one of us matters. It is as though we are cells in the Body of God, and being such we can never be separated from that which can bring us clarity of Mind, Openness of Heart and Wings to our Spirit.

Some of these Angel communications were, how should I say, dictated, or rather, eloquently shared with me so that I could pass on their wisdom and depth with others. Some of what I share are experiences that helped me "feel" their presence, which allowed me to know that we are far more important in the grand scheme of life than we have dared to know in the past.

Each of us has an important role to play in the evolution of Humankind. We are the solution to saving ourselves from ourselves. But first, we must take only one tiny step in the direction of wonder. The door that is opened a mere crack is no longer closed. Each experience allows the doors of our hearts to open a bit wider, bit by bit, minute by minute and hour by hour, until we come to the last hour, minute and second of our life, and truly know the gift that we have been given. Let's open our minds and hearts to new possibilities... and know that we are more than we appear.

But first, let me share a bit about myself and how I began to understand that Divine Beings are all around... even in our darkest hours.

the Heart of the matter is what matters

THE ANGELS AND ME

ANSWERING AN UNANSWERABLE PRAYER

*"Give light
and the people
will find their own way."*

Motto of Scripps-Howard Newspapers

It's a funny thing when you think that you know something and you later realize that you really know nothing about the subject at all. You get stopped in your tracks, looking back at all the times you were "sure" you knew something, and then looking again, you realize that you may have only experienced a tiny fraction for a moment and you believed that you knew the whole. We humans do that so quickly and so often. We believe that things we were taught are absolutes. If we make one minor misstep that action might prevent further knowledge from squeezing its way in. Perfection, as taught by Dominican nuns, was at best a difficult task.

The notion of a prayer being heard was one that I had grappled with for many years. Oh sure, I was taught how to pray, and I could recite a prayer like all the other kids in my parochial school, but knowing a prayer and *knowing* a prayer are two very different things. And then, you have the vague concept of having a prayer being answered. Does that ever really happen? As a child I would sometimes worry that if I did not recall the correct intonation and have the proper reverence when reciting a prayer, somehow I would incur an unbearable wrath sometime in the future. If I missed a word in a prayer, or haphazardly thought about other things while praying, I could have been adding yet another "venial" sin to the already marked up chalkboard of my little Catholic soul. Some nuns and priests were great at messing with my concept of God. Then why did I believe, or rather know, that they were wrong and that Angels and God were much kinder than any person who represented them could be?

Many times in my childhood and early adolescence I would pray; actually it was more like plead to both God and the Angels, and it seemed hard to comprehend that they were listening. Confusing concepts were planted in my mind in my early days of parochial school. I never fully grasped how my eating vegetables (peas, especially) could help a child in an unknown land go to bed with a full tummy. And what were "pagan babies" anyway? I recall that we had to dutifully collect money for those less fortunate children, but I never comprehended how my measly little box of pennies could "save" them from their misfortune.

However, I do remember that I would feel lightness in my heart if I said a prayer or imagined another child smiling as I dropped my pennies into the red box marked "Pagan Babies." It all seemed so confusing when we were taught to "love one another" but warned to stay away from the "public school kids." I somehow knew that something was not right when we were asked to collect pennies for one group of kids, and shun another because they did not attend our school.

Grownups, even the ones with pious names and black and white garments, could be very unkind in their delivery of "God's Message." Deep within me I had a feeling that they were talking to the wrong Angels, or at the very least, misinterpreting their messages. Angels never said that you couldn't touch a tiny piece of host, even if it got stuck on the roof of your mouth, and that if you did, you had yet another chalk mark on your "venial sin list."

Boy, sometimes my head would spin from all the rules.

Then one day, the rug was yanked out from under me, and all that I knew about God and the Angels fell hopelessly to Earth, and for a time, prayers felt empty and useless.

Our brother Brian had Duchene Muscular Dystrophy, a cruel disease that robs its host of the ability to use muscles. One by one his muscles weakened until, at the age of fifteen, he no longer had the strength to cough, even to save his own life. Muscular Dystrophy was a pallor that hung over our family, and one day, it literally took his and our breath away. Even though the disease took his strength, it never diminished the beauty and strength of his spirit. Before long, I began to understand the real purpose of prayer. In the past, I had used the action of prayer to ask for something to be changed; but it was much later that I learned that prayer was meant to help us cope with the inevitability of change by bringing love and awareness into our lives.

Brian was a happy spirit, with an incredible mind for facts, dates, and history who loved life and especially loved his family. He was a gift to us, an Angel in our midst, and we were fortunate enough to know it. The prognosis for his type of dystrophy is a lifespan of less than twenty years. This was the case with Brian. His life was taken one month shy of his sixteenth birthday, the last week of his junior high school career.

Brian was determined to live his life, regardless of the hindrance that dystrophy imposed upon his body, and he had a magnificent singing voice. He sang a solo at our sister Judy's wedding. He never allowed the severe scoliosis that impaired his lung capacity to deter him from his joy of singing. So impressive was his voice that he sang a solo in the school concert just days before his death. He was able to participate in the first evening's performance, but due to complications of respiratory problems, he was not able to be at the second performance. A cold could lead to pneumonia, and ultimately death.

The choir director, knowing of Brian's breathing difficulties, called our mom to see if it were possible for Brian to be in attendance that night, even if he couldn't sing. Unfortunately my mother had to tell her that he could not be there. The director shared with my mom in that telephone conversation that a special award was to be given to Brian that evening - an Inspirational Trophy on behalf of the entire student body. Thanking her for this wonderful acknowledgement, my mother promised to let Brian know, and we would have a family celebration in lieu of the concert.

Later that day my dad had carried Brian to the bathroom where he started to cough. The cough brought up phlegm that caught in his throat. Brian began to choke. In a panic my dad screamed, "Elaine, come here!" Both my mother and I share the same name. Thinking he was calling for me and hearing the fear in his voice, we all ran to the bedroom, where my father had brought Brian by this time. It just so happened that there were six of us in the house that day - Dad, Mom, my sister Chris, her friend Sharon, who happened to be a nurse, Brian and myself. I got to the room first, finding my dad standing next to Brian's bed. Brian was slumped forward.

As my father raised him up, I saw that his face was blue, his eyes bulging with a look of total fear on his face. He looked directly at me, and God help me I don't know how he did it, he cried out, "Don't let me die!" Within a moment of that plea, he was unconscious.

In a panic, my father asked if he should call an ambulance

Sharon said that there was no time for that and that he had to be taken to the hospital immediately. After wrapping Brian in a blanket, our father carried him to the car and placed his limp body in the arms of our mother. As they left the driveway, my fear was beyond measure. On the drive to the hospital, my brother died in the arms of his mother. That was not the end.

Upon arrival at the hospital, the emergency room team began CPR. They did it so many times that they broke most of his ribs. After several cardiac arrests, and several resuscitations, he was finally put on a respirator in the ICU. His poor body, worn out from the struggle with Muscular Dystrophy, lay in the ICU bed, broken and bruised. His brain had been deprived of oxygen far too long and my parents were given this information. Mom and Dad had to make the decision to shut off the machine that was breathing his breath for him. Three days after being admitted through the emergency room, our sweet brother Brian had died. It was June 3, 1968.

The night that he went to the hospital I remember lying on the pullout bed in the basement, desperately trying to bargain with God. I promised to be a better helper for Brian. I would not complain if he needed the urinal or if I had to help him brush his teeth. I won't mind if I have to exercise his legs. I won't complain about anything if you don't make him suffer, and if at all possible, bring him back, whole and alive. Going to school was almost impossible.

The morning of June 3, 1968, my older sister Chris was sitting on the bed waiting for me to wake up. The moment my eyes opened she told me that Brian was dead. I honestly don't remember too much after that moment. The inevitable happened. There is nothing one can do to prepare for the moment that you know someone that you love has died. It is a burden that can break a human heart. I numbly went through the motions of helping with whatever needed to be done that day. The air was so thick with sadness it was difficult to breathe.

Brian was always a generous spirit and his generosity continued even after his death. In a private conversation, he had told Mom that the only part of his body not affected by Muscular Dystrophy were his beautiful eyes, and if possible, he would want someone else to have them. He was generous and loving to the end. His eyes were donated, giving someone else the gift of sight.

I remember the difficulty of that hot summer day, having to walk into the funeral home for the first time. There was a young man named Bob who was the greeter at the funeral home. Bob was not much older than myself, and had seen too many sad faces pass through those doors. Somehow his kind, knowing, smile seemed to ease my steps as I walked across the threshold of the Thayer Funeral Home. I vividly recall my brother Mike and I walking up to Brian's casket, my trembling body barely able to bring me there.

The funeral home was crowded with a constant stream of people coming though the door. At one point, the line could not be contained within the walls of the funeral home, and at least one hundred people waited quietly outside for their chance to pay their respects. There was a moment that I shall never forget, when the choir director, along with the entire school choir, walked into the funeral parlor holding in her hand the Inspirational Trophy that was to be presented to Brian by the student body of Dunkel Junior High School at the choir recital. Instead, they brought it to the funeral home and gave it to our parents. Mom placed it on his casket. It was a moment of great pride mixed with unspeakable sadness.

The morning of Brian's funeral, I had a very vivid dream that revisited me many times since. It was my first lucid dream that I can remember. It was also precognitive. In my dream I was walking down the stairs in our tri-level house and looking into the dining room I could see the entire family at the table, joking and happy and in a celebrating mood. I noticed immediately that Brian and Mom were sitting together at the head of the table. In unison they stood, both glowing in white light, both smiling broadly. What was significant was the fact that Brian was standing! For the last five years of his life, he had been confined to a wheelchair. The implications of this message kindly evaded my understanding.

As I opened my eyes that morning, my sister Chris was again sitting on the side of my bed. Again she broke unspeakable news, "Bobby Kennedy was killed last night," was all that she said. It was June 5, 1968. Life would never be the same again.

Within the next few weeks, our brother John would graduate from high school and our parents would host our sister Dianne's long planned June wedding. Our parents did not wish to postpone living. Death was a part of life.

make kindness a part of
everything you do.
no smile is ever wasted.
no thought or
prayer will go unheard.

WATCHING AN ANGEL

"No man should think himself a zero,
and think he can do nothing
about the state of the world."

Bernard M. Baruch

If there was one thing that our mom knew about, it was love. She exuded it all of the time. She had an uncanny way of knowing when someone was in need of a little kindness, and she would effortlessly share the abundance of love within her.

As kids, she would take us on wonderful adventures. We would go to the theatre, the museum, to the beach, on a picnic or to the zoo. She loved to have fun and learn at the same time. One of our favorite summertime excursions was an amusement park called Bob-Lo Island. Mom would gather enough food to feed her small army, with usually enough to spare, if someone was in need. Mom and her sister Gloria were very close, and the cousins were often together during summer vacations.

One such trip to Bob-Lo Island is a testament to her caring heart. This particular trip occurred before Brian's death. As usual, we were jammed into the station wagon, each anxious to be on the Bob-Lo boat and spend the hour playing and dancing our way there. On this occasion, with Brian in his wheelchair, we camped out on the lower deck of the boat, with Mom and Gloria keeping a watchful eye on us.

Mom seemed to have special radar for troubled souls. I remember sitting near my brother as my mother got up from her chair and walked over to a young uniformed man who was leaning against the railing of the boat, watching the Detroit skyline drift by. She gently stated to him that he looked as if he was alone, and invited him to spend the day with our family. "No one," she said, "should have to be alone in an amusement park." Somehow she convinced him to join our motley crew. I remember watching his face throughout the day, seemingly changing from the sad, burdened heart that I had noticed when I first saw him to someone who somehow felt as if he belonged, if only for a day.

About a week later, this same young, handsome soldier was standing at our front door with a bouquet of flowers in his hand. We were happy, yet surprised, to see him. He wanted to thank Mom for her kindness to him that day. She never pried into the cause of his distress as he stood at the railing that day and he wanted her to know that on that day she had saved his life. He had spent his life in foster homes, and when he was old enough he joined the military. This was his first leave, and he knew he had no home to go to. He felt completely alone leaning against that railing, wondering how best to end his life, since he felt he had no life at all.

But an angel with a full picnic basket and a heart full of unconditional love stopped him. That angel was my mother.

*When you touch
another's heart
with love —
soul touches
soul*

MY WOUNDING

*"The moments of our greatest trials
can be like irons in a fire,
tempering the heart with the
heat of seemingly endless grief."*

Author Unknown

The following year, on August 13, 1969, our parents hosted the wedding of Chris and Jack. Chris was the third daughter to be married in as many years and the wedding was planned after Jack returned safely from Vietnam. After the wedding, the newlyweds were off on their honeymoon and things settled for a moment. Mom was scheduled to have surgery the last week of August 1969. Within a month's time, she moved her mother-in-law and sister-in-law from Detroit to Farmington, hosted a third wedding for my sister Chris and prepared her home and herself for surgery. She must have been exhausted.

The morning of her hospital admission, she asked me to come into her bedroom and she began to show me where all of the important documents were kept. Insurance policies, birth certificates, as well as other important papers were explained. She wanted me to know exactly where they were. Knowing these things seemed very unsettling to me. One by one she showed me where every pre-purchased gift was, who it was for, and what the occasion might be. To help me keep track, each box had a little sheet of paper with the recipient's name and information on it.

She had a wonderful way of remembering special occasions for others.

She asked me to sit with her on the bed as she brought over her jewelry box and put it on the bed between us. As we sat together, she reminisced about each piece of jewelry, the good and the costume, telling me who gave it to her and why. One treasure was a large snowflake made of inexpensive "diamonds" which my sister Chris had purchased for her at a garage sale. To her, it was like the Crown Jewels.

She then reached inside and brought out the silver charm bracelet that we had given to her the summer before for our parents' twenty-fifth wedding anniversary. It had the first charm Dad had ever given her, along with one that commemorated their anniversary. Nestled between these two special charms was one for each of her children, with our names engraved on heart-shaped charms. "This," she said, "I will bring with me to the hospital, because it will be the last time I will ever wear it." Stunned by her words, I asked her what she meant. She just repeated her words softly and gave me a hug. I had a terrible feeling as we left home to go to the hospital that plagued me for a very long time.

Mom had decided that she was going to buy something that day that she had always wanted to buy but never did. Even though she had pretty red hair, it was very fine, and she had always wanted thicker hair. So, we went to the millinery department at Hudson's and she tried on every red-haired wig. She talked and laughed with the saleswoman who took care of her. Mom settled on one, which was very near her own red hair color, just much thicker and with many curls. We all had fun laughing and trying on hats and wigs. We were there for quite some time and she promised the sales clerk that she would return to that department to show her how it looked.

After lunch, we headed to the hospital. She was scheduled to have bladder suspension surgery the following day. Dad had arranged for her to have a private hospital room so that she would be able to rest without too much interruption, allowing her to recuperate quicker. We laughed and felt the love that was so much a part of her being. Yet, her words to me that morning in her bedroom echoed in my mind.

That evening, I stayed home with my dad to be sure that he was all right. Arrangements had been made for my younger sister and brother to stay at our Aunt Gloria's house. The afternoon of surgery, it was reported that everything was fine; and my plans were once again to be home with my dad, to be certain that he ate and was not alone.

My brother's girlfriend and I went to the hospital the day after the surgery. As we arrived in the room, Dad was sitting quietly in a chair, with his ever-present newspaper. I walked to the side of the bed and quietly spoke her name. Mom was aware that I was there with her, but was still sedated from the surgery and she had a very hard time focusing. She took my hand in hers and told me, "Honey, always remember that I love you." I told her that I loved her too and I cried when it was time to leave her. Something was gnawing at me and I felt concern as I left the room.

That night I was planning to stay at home with my dad. I didn't want him to be alone in the house. My older brother Mike had gone to spend the night at a friend's house, and my younger sister Maureen and my baby brother Paul were at my Aunt Gloria and Uncle Al's home. Reluctantly, my aunt convinced me to come and spend the night along with the other kids. I did not wish to go there that evening, thinking that I needed to keep my dad company.

My sister, Dianne, who is a nurse, had wanted to take care of Mom, and had come down from Lansing after the surgery to be her private duty nurse. Dianne worked well into the night, leaving at approximately 10:00 pm to return home. She was scheduled to work at her regular nursing position the following day. During the late hours of the night, our mother passed away.

That evening I was walking down the street with my cousin and her friends, and all of the other girls were complaining about their mothers. I couldn't join in their discussion, because I truly had nothing to complain about. My thoughts and prayers were with my mother and her recovery. And there was a nagging fear of her words about her bracelet.

Sometime during the night as I lay on a cot in my cousin's bedroom, I rolled over and as if in a dream, I remember seeing my Aunt Gloria, Uncle Al, cousin Rick, and my Uncle Jimmy standing at the door of the bedroom looking in. Thinking that I was dreaming, I rolled over and went back to sleep. This, however, was no dream. During the night there had been a power outage, and Uncle Jim, my mom's youngest brother, had to come over, since the telephones were not working. They had stood together at the door wondering how they were going to break news to us that would shatter our world.

The following morning I got up as usual, had breakfast with my cousins, aunt, uncle, and my two younger siblings. My uncle was referred to as the "Polish Prince" in our family and we joked about "Polish meetings." I always would help with dishes; so after cleaning up, I vividly remember my aunt asking me to call the other kids in; she needed to talk to us. I stood at the bottom of the stairs and laughingly called up to the others to come down, because we were having a "Polish meeting."

We all came into the family room and Gloria asked me to sit next to her. Uncle Al was sitting across the room from me and all of a sudden I saw him start to cry. I had never seen a man cry this way before and my heart began to pound. Gloria put her arm around me and simply said, "Your mom is dead." Paul, in his three-year-old innocence, just continued to play on the floor as my vision began to fade. I remember being able to see only what was directly in front of me. I told her that she was wrong, and she repeated her words. My already fragile world was being shattered again, and I wondered how I would ever be able to bring all my broken pieces back together.

Walking through the doors of the funeral home all too soon after my brother Brian's funeral was one of the most difficult moments of my life. The same sweet face of Bob greeted me at the funeral home door.

As is the custom, the immediate family is given private time to be with their loved one before other family and friends begin to arrive. We walked into the same room where Brian had been a little over a year before, with her coffin resting at the opposite end of the room. Approaching yet another casket made my thirteen-year-old legs feel like those of a ninety-year-old woman. Each step was painful.

Only a little over a year before, my brother Mike and I walked up together, supporting each other as we walked together toward an uncertain future. Now we were doing it again. From a distance I could see her turquoise dress that she had worn to her anniversary party. I could see her soft red curly hair as her head rested on the white pillow. Her soft freckled skin lacked the glow that she brought into a room. You wonder where the soul has gone when you the lack the presence of someone you love so dearly.

In March 1970, our Grandpa Vic, Mom's father, would die. His decline was rapid after the loss of his beautiful daughter. He went from being perfectly healthy to dementia seemingly overnight. Then in April 1970, our father lost his mother, Grandma Hughes, to a massive heart attack. I feared that the deaths would never end. In twenty-three months we lost Brian, Mom, Grandpa and Grandma.

My life changed dramatically. Three years later our father, a widower with eight surviving children, married a widow with seven children of her own. They remained married for thirty-two years, eventually dying one year and one day apart.

Ten years later, at the age of twenty-three, I married my husband, Rich Grohman, who I had known since grade school. Before long we had two beautiful children, Elaine and Brian, named after my mother and brother. They are the treasured angels in my life. For many years we lived a fairly typical life until one day the Angels stepped directly in my path and my life would never be the same.

A MOMENT TO REMEMBER

*"The human spirit is stronger than
anything that can happen to it."*

George C. Scott

There are times where the spiritual world needs to rock ours in order to get our attention so that we begin to see what is truly going on. My experience, the one that awakened a curiosity deep within me that I couldn't resist seeking further, began in a quiet setting in the home of my dying aunt. Gloria was my mother's younger sister. She was in the end stages of diabetes, having been hospitalized due to kidney failure. She was signed onto hospice care and sent home. It was apparent that her time was slipping away. The hospital staff gave a prognosis of two weeks. She lasted closer to six. It is truly between God and the individual when their life will end.

My cousin, her daughter and caregiver, was in need of a bit of respite from caring for her dying mother, struggling with the emotional turmoil that caregiving can create, on top of having estranged family members coming into town to be together. Although the dying process can be lengthy, it is a blessing when those that need to make amends are given the opportunity to do just that, to the best of their ability.

One particular day, I suggested to my cousin that she take a break; go do something for herself, assuring her that I would sit with her mother until her return. As I sat in the small room at the bedside of my aunt, I was fairly sure that her time on this Earth was rapidly coming to an end. She had been in and out of consciousness that day, and for the most part had been non-responsive. I simply sat by her bed holding her hand, telling her that if she wanted to go that all would be fine. I thanked her for all that she had done for us and assured her that we would help one another. She lay motionless, seemingly unaware of my presence with her. Then as if a light switch was flipped on she opened her eyes and said, "I see my sister." I simply replied, "Then, honey, you go to her, because she will take good care of you." That sister was my mother who had died twenty-seven years before.

After those words were spoken, she gently closed her eyes. At that moment, I felt a very tangible movement in the room. I can only describe it as a "whooshing" feeling, gently moving back and forth from side to side. It was a momentary event, but one that would change my life. There were no fans blowing or open windows, yet there was a distinct movement. I still can feel the tingle of electricity throughout my body as I recall feeling this movement, this intangible, yet palpable, movement in the room. I now know that I was privileged to feel her spirit begin to separate from her physical body. As it turned out, it was just a day or two later that she passed away.

This was a very moving moment for me, since her only sister, my mother, had died when I was thirteen years old, when she was only forty-seven. My aunt and my mother were very close and I always knew that my aunt was never quite the same after the passing of her dear sister. My world changed forever on that day.

After my aunt's passing, funeral arrangements had to be made. I found myself often thinking about the experience of the events in her room that day. From the time that she was discharged from the hospital, she began to receive hospice care. I was very moved by the care that she received, along with the care that the family received. Throughout the difficult time of impending death, hospice care and the marvelous people that provided it made a lasting impression on me.

Since my aunt was not a particularly religious woman, she had not been a practicing member of her church for some time. With this knowledge, although her funeral mass was held at a church, my cousin elected to ask the hospice spiritual care practitioner if she would speak at the funeral home. I asked her if I could speak and she kindly accepted the offer. After the evening service the hospice chaplain came up to me and asked if I had ever considered working for hospice. Apparently the words I spoke to express my feelings for my aunt and her last week of life struck a cord with her. And, to be truthful, her question brought the idea squarely in front of my eyes. Did I have any interest in hospice care? Could I do it? Would I want to?

It just so happened that there was a Hospice Home being built directly across the street from the grocery store that I frequented. Every time I drove to the store and saw the construction reaching completion, there was a nagging thought in my mind: "There is something here that you need to investigate, Elaine, don't put it off." Well, after many moments of doubt, I finally made the decision to call to find out what was required to become a hospice volunteer. Little did I know that the kind woman that I spoke with that day, and who would train me as a hospice volunteer, would be the woman that I would replace in that position within the year.

only love will
change the
World
starting with my heart

THIS IS WHAT IT IS

"Let us watch well our beginnings,
and results will manage themselves."

Alexander Clark

Hospice training gave me a very thorough understanding of the hospice and palliative care model of medicine and I began to volunteer my time at the Hospice Home. This, I reasoned, would allow me the opportunity to assist as I had the time, with no long-term commitment to one individual. As time progressed, I realized that I was in exactly the right place at the right time.

I will not tell you that this is an easy line of work. But I will say that it is without a doubt one of the most rewarding things that I have ever done. I was privileged to step into the most intimate time of peoples' lives, sharing memories, sorrows, joys, and always tremendous insights, and for those times I am eternally grateful. Because of those sacred times with patients, my life's work was being paved for me.

My curiosity about energy healing and opening my intuition was piqued once again when I met a massage therapist. I noticed as she worked on me that there were times when she did not touch my body, but I could definitely feel something. I just wasn't quite sure what that something was. Quite often I would see very bright colors and distinct images in my mind's eye. Intrigued, we would often spend a great deal of time talking about what she was doing. I wanted to know how I could learn about this thing called Energy Healing. Her recommendation was training in Polarity Therapy. Before too long, I was enrolled in a two-and-a-half-year course of study in Polarity Therapy. I soon discovered that I was again in the right place at the right time. Since I was volunteering in a medical model, and seeing firsthand what was occurring in the dying process, Polarity was the perfect fit.

Dr. Randolph Stone developed Polarity Therapy in the 1920s. Being a country doctor, he tended to all of the needs of his patients - the Body, the Mind and the Spirit. Having been designed by a physician, Polarity Therapy is very physiologically based. My education in this unique energy of the body and its organ systems proved to be an excellent entry into Energy Medicine.

Considering the fact that I had entered a medical model of end-of-life-care, my beginning to understand energy from an academic, yet tactile, modality assisted me greatly in understanding the energy of the dying process. Yet, the most profound understanding was the changing of the human spirit when one has knowledge that his/her life is coming to its conclusion. The energy of the physical body is beautiful and awe-inspiring, but the unique and mystical spirit and mind can grow and mature in beautiful ways, even as the physical body declines.

I am always amazed at the clever ways in which God tries to help us learn. In class, we would learn about the various organ systems, learning to distinguish the unique energy patterns of the circulatory, pulmonary, digestive and nervous systems. For example, we might learn how to palpate the energy of the pulmonary system (lungs), and the following week I would have several patients dying of lung cancer. It was as if God was saying, "This is what it is, and this is what it looks like. Are you paying attention?" Time, and time again, I was shown how to sense and feel the energy of a physical problem so that I could have a deeper understanding of what was happening in the physical body. I am not a medically trained person. I was, however, in a medical model that many in allopathic medicine shied away from, namely the inevitable – death.

I later went on to become an Associate Polarity Practitioner, a Certified Healing Touch Practitioner, an Angel Therapy Practitioner and the developer and teacher of a powerful energetic modality called Sacred Geometry and Energy Medicine.

So much of what I had wondered about since the time of my brother, mother and aunt's deaths was beginning to open up in profound and astonishing ways. I would soon know that it was possible to have contact from those who had passed from this life, and from the Angels that I had always prayed to. Were they truly intermediaries that could assist us with understanding what our lives were truly about? It was in this environment of hospice care that I truly began to believe and understand the importance that the Angels held in my life, opening doors that most people believed are not only closed, but locked from us, forever. I would learn how wrong we had been.

Time and again, I was privileged to stand at a bedside while completely lucid people would talk to me about the "others" standing in their room or beside their beds with us. The Spirits were palpable, loving, patient and ever present and I was awed by what I was fortunate enough to witness.

Regardless of their religious background, more people than not spoke to me of the beauty and wonder that they saw that served to ease their fear of dying.

FORGIVENESS

"One can be very happy without demanding
that others should agree with him."

Johann Wolfgang von Goethe

One day, as I was working in the hospice facility, there was an elderly man whom I will call Joe who was admitted to the facility. He was dying of metastatic lung cancer, and he was a very angry man. His condition had deteriorated to a state that is sometimes referred to as "failure to die." A person's body seems to be functioning on air alone, no food in, no excrements out, multi-system failure, yet there is still a struggling for life. Often there is a spiritual or emotional struggle going on, and I was about to witness it.

As I was getting ready to knock on his door the nurse pulled me aside. She quietly said, "He is really angry, so you may not want to go in there. Why not let the chaplain and social worker take care of him?" I assured her that I would be all right, and if he didn't want to talk, I would certainly respect that. Perhaps he had the right to be angry, and he wasn't angry with me so I thought I would give it a try.

I knocked on his door and asked if I could come in. "Why the hell not, no one else will talk to me," was his reply. As he sat alone in his room, I could feel the tension of his abrasive personality, which seemed to have been used as his shield throughout his life. He even looked like a tough character. I quietly intro-

34

duced myself and asked if I could sit down. "Sure, why not?" was his reply. As we sat together I asked him to tell me about himself, what was important to him, and slowly his demeanor began to soften as he began to tell me about his life. "Damn it, I am dying, and I want to get it over with. I don't have anything to live for and I am really angry that God won't let me die."

I quietly listened to him as he unleashed his anger at God and the world in general. He felt that he had been treated unfairly and that his life was not as he had wanted. He was angry, and he didn't care who knew it. Without warning, I began to hear a voice repeat a message over and over in my mind. "Tell him he must forgive his brother, tell him he must forgive his brother, tell him he must forgive his brother." I discreetly looked around the room, trying to comprehend who was talking to me. Again, it repeated, "Tell him he must forgive his brother."

The thought would not go away so I finally asked, "Joe, do you have a brother?" He looked a bit startled and said, "Yes, I have a brother, that son of a bitch." Oh boy! Still feeling the prodding from the unseen voice, I continued. "Joe, do you think that you could forgive your brother?" Again, with a look of indignation he said, "How the hell can I do that, he has been dead for forty years?" We continued to talk and I could still feel that there was urgency to this message and that things could finally be brought to the light of day. "Joe, do you want to talk about what happened that made you so angry at your brother?" I asked. Sitting for a moment it seemed that his mind went back in time. He looked at me with some anger still in his eyes and said, "I really can't re-member..." his voice trailing off into his memories.

There was an unseen force in the room, one that I would come to know over time. This Force was opening the door to heal a wounded heart, or perhaps more than one. Joe's brother had been dead for forty years, but the event that caused the rift had happened perhaps fifteen years prior to his brother's death. With tears in his eyes Joe realized that he had been angry with his brother for over fifty years, and now, as his own life was drawing to a close, he realized that he couldn't remember why.

As we talked, he acknowledged that he has spoken badly about his brother, perhaps influencing others' thoughts of him, and certainly causing a separation between the two of them. Joe began to understand that his anger was the veil through which he viewed all the people in his life, and that it did not have to be that way. Tears began to show in his eyes when he asked, "Do you think it is still possible to forgive my brother? And I think I should ask for forgiveness too." "Absolutely, just say it, either to yourself or out loud. Either way, I am sure that it will be heard," was my reply.

Soon it was time for me to go home for the day and I thanked Joe for being willing to share all of this with me. As I started to leave he asked if he could give me a hug, and we hugged one another warmly. I smiled and asked Joe if I could come back to visit him again. "I wish you would," he softly said as I walked out the door.

The following day I learned that Joe had died that night, and I was concerned that perhaps I had done something that may have caused his death. As I spoke to one of the nurses I shared my concern. "Don't worry, Elaine, it is a good thing. You didn't cause it, you helped to allow it." My heart was grateful as I thanked Joe for the honor of being a part of his life.

*Not by words
alone do
we reveal who we
Are.*

BUILD A QUIET MIND

"Every spirit builds itself a house,
and beyond its house a world,
and beyond
its world a heaven.
Know then that world exists for you."

Ralph Waldo Emerson

Prayer should not be an act of pleading for one thing or another. Prayer is a conversation. We have been taught that as we pray, our intentions and words drift out somewhere into the ethers, and, if we are good, we might get a message back, but who knew when or how.

My thoughts of prayers are no longer confined to a ritual act of reciting words, but rather is an open communication, from one loving friend to another: one between the Angels, God and me. We as humans aren't quite used to that concept of communication. We often do not share the full story. Our communication is influenced by our emotional response to people and events, often tainting what is really happening.

The true act of prayer is to open your heart, and therefore your whole being so that you can give and receive at the same time, and that is, after all, the essence of true conversation. One speaks and the other listens, and hopefully comprehends what is being shared. Most humans are terribly poor communicators. Individuals, or groups of individuals, need to be open-minded for full communication to take place. Often, we don't fully pay attention, and thereby misinterpret what is being said. Or worse, we are so set in our ways that anything other than what we want is perceived as a threat. That is not communication, that is posturing.

When we truly begin to communicate we do not simply listen to the words we hear. Rather, we use the totality of our senses to receive the information. We perceive body language, intonation, expression, and even feel the "energy" of the person, often without being consciously aware of all the information we are receiving.

Yet with Angelic communication, when you are in conversation with them, it is more often like a movement through waves of time, and one must have a quiet mind to pay attention to what is occurring. A quiet mind is not a simple mind. The quiet mind allows many things in and can begin, over time, to discern the meanings of the whispers, just as if you were outside on a beautiful night and could hear the sounds of nature. The quieter you are, the more you could hear and the more you would hear the more easily you could discern the voice of an owl from the song of a dove.

Allow me to share some of the Angel's wisdom, and how they have touched my life in big and small ways. They are ever present, ever patient and ever watchful, quietly standing guard as we open our senses and hearts in unimaginable ways.

SURROUNDED BY GRACE

"Thou hast seen nothing yet."

Miguel De Cervantes

The times that I have spent with clients have helped me to become more aware, giving me the opportunity to help them find their health, in whatever degree it resides, and invite it to be embraced by the whole. As I work with clients I ask them to pay attention to everything that they are experiencing. The client is there for a reason. Most importantly, I believe, they are there to discover themselves. Therefore, I speak to them throughout the energy treatment, asking them to pay attention to everything. How does your body feel? What do you notice? Is there tension, relaxation or pain? Notice, pay attention! The job of a healer or an intuitive is to help the person recognize him or herself. Sounds silly, but how many times do you actually recognize what your body is telling you?

It is never appropriate for a healer, whether a physician, nurse, social worker or energy healer, to become the authority figure in the relationship between the client and themselves. Certainly, one may be more knowledgeable about a particular subject, but it is important that a client become an equal partner, never giving up his or her own important role in healing. The fact is that the client is the only one that can do the healing. We surely can assist with our own expertise, but ultimately it is the individual who must go home to their own personal place of healing. It is essential that the current model of the healing relationship change since it has clearly not helped people to heal themselves. I believe the best relationship is one of support and nurturance that does not require abdication of one's own healing resources.

This vehicle, your human body, is constantly trying to help your spirit grow, expand and become aware. How many times do we ignore pain, discomfort or that little nagging thought that is trying to help us wake up? All too often, I suspect. I am no exception to this, but I am learning. We not only ignore what our body is telling us, but we ignore what our heart is telling us. I think that many people are not willing to even look at the goodness that is within them. Having been raised Catholic myself, I had the misguided belief that we should not acknowledge our gifts and talents, but to simply go about humbly through life. We foolishly believe that we are not important enough for "special help" or assistance from the Divine. Poignantly, God can use others to get our attention.

Preceding my work at hospice, I had heard a radio interview of a woman named Judith Orloff, M.D. Intrigued by the conversation, I heard that she was giving a lecture at a local, well-known church, of which I had never attended. I decided to attend the lecture that was scheduled for that evening. I not only decided to go, but I could honestly say that I felt as though I had to go, that there was a message for me that I needed to hear.

It was a very cold winter evening, so I bundled up and made the drive to the event. Typically, whenever I attend a lecture, I enjoy sitting as close to the front as possible. I distinctly remember as I walked down the aisle to see if there were any seats near the front, three women, sitting in the first row, turned around as I was walking toward the seats behind them. One woman in particular made eye contact with me, and I simply smiled, assuming that she was looking for another person to join her small group.

If you have never had the opportunity to hear or read Dr. Judith Orloff's work, I would suggest that you do. She is a brilliant psychiatrist, author, intuitive and a blessed human being. Her lecture that evening was to discuss her most current book at the time, *Second Sight*. The lecture involved her experiences of being a young, gifted intuitive, with the ability to "know," at a very early age, things that a child would not know. In other words, she had visitations of deceased loved ones, and had the ability to know, at a deep level, things that her young mind could not understand. Her lecture touched me deeply.

After the lecture, I stood in line to purchase her book and have it autographed. There were many people waiting for an autograph, so I just stood patiently awaiting my turn. As I stood in line, the woman who had turned around at the beginning of the evening came up to speak to me. I smiled as she approached, and she said, "I hope you won't mind if I say this but as you walked into the auditorium I felt compelled to turn around, and I didn't know why. I saw you walk down the aisle, and you were glowing the most beautiful pink light. It felt as though that pink light forced me to turn around. I don't know who you are, but your energy is very strong and peaceful." Well, I didn't know what to say. I had never had anyone say anything like that to me before. So, I simply said, "Thank you."

Little, by little, I was getting closer to Dr. Orloff. As I stood in front of the table where she was signing books, she looked up at me for a moment with a warm smile and then looked down again. Briefly, she looked up again as if she was looking behind me. She asked my name, and then wrote an inscription on the page. Before I walked away, she looked at me again and said, very sweetly, "The Blessed Mother is standing right behind you."

I was shocked, and more than a little awed. Being raised a

Catholic, the Blessed Mother had always been important to me, and I would pray to her often, especially after the death of my own mother. In her lecture, Dr. Orloff mentioned that she had been raised Jewish, and in my ignorance I assumed that she would not know that much about the Blessed Mother. Silly of me. That was the second time that someone had told me that Our Lady was with me.

In a moment, I will relate that story, but to continue. I smiled, and thanked her for her words, and for autographing the book for me. As I walked away a bit stunned, I read the inscription. She wrote, "To Elaine, a woman of hope." Before too long, that message would send chills of confirmation throughout my body. Shortly after attending Dr. Orloff's lecture, events unfolded that brought me to be a hospice volunteer. I can still see the words in my mind's eye as I was sitting in the volunteer training class. I opened the volunteer manual; and the very first line of the introduction said, "The meaning of hospice is hope." I was being asked to be a woman of hope. What did that mean?

During my hospice training I was given yet another gift that helped to open my eyes and heart to new territory. While listening to the trainer, I became mesmerized by a magnificent violet light that was emanating from the crown of her head. I looked around at the other participants in the training to see if anyone else seemed to be noticing this strange sight. That didn't appear to be the case. I looked around the room trying to locate the source of this beautiful light. There wasn't any. The light was coming from her!

Since my childhood I had been able to see very soft light around people. Nothing prepared me for what I was witnessing that evening. As she spoke, the love and respect that she had for the dignity of the dying was opening her crown chakra, allowing the beautiful energy of that center to be visible. I felt blessed and awed that I was being given the opportunity to see this amazing sight. It would occur many times in the future.

I would like to tell you a little story about the first time I was given a message about the Blessed Mother. I had heard a radio interview of a very interesting woman who was discussing how she had recently helped a woman who thought that she had spirits in her home. The guest on the show was a woman named Karen. Yet again, I felt as though I needed to see this woman. During the conversation she mentioned that she did private readings. My fortieth birthday was that week so I made an appointment as a gift to myself. The appointment was scheduled to take place the day before my birthday.

It had been a very long time since I had had a psychic reading, the first being when I was about twenty years old. I nervously kept busy that morning until it was time for me to go to Ann Arbor to meet with Karen. I told no one of this appointment, this was my fortieth birthday gift to myself. I prayed the whole time I was driving to the appointment. At one point, I began to say the rosary out loud to myself. I remember laughing out loud hoping that I would not offend the Blessed Mother, since I could not remember how the decades of the rosary went. I said out loud, "Hope you don't mind, but I am just going to say it as I remember, no offense." I literally laughed out loud at myself as I drove westbound on M-14 talking and praying out loud.

Before long I was in front of Karen's home. Nervously, I approached the door. She answered with enthusiasm, invited me to have a seat as she finished a phone call. She invited me into a small room that she used to do her readings. I sat down, with her seated directly across from me. The first thing she said was, "Do you always travel with this many angels?" And before I could respond, she continued. "There is someone very important here, and I do not see her very often, so this is special. She says, thank you for the prayers."

She then told me that the Blessed Mother was standing behind me and that her energy was enfolding my own. My whole body was tingling. I laughed and cried at the same time as I told Karen what had happened in the car on the way to her home. She told me that the Blessed Mother was listening to my prayers and wanted to be sure that I knew that. Well, I definitely knew it from that moment on.

Since the time of my mother's death in August of 1969, I had always prayed that I would be able to see or hear from my mom someday. During the reading, my mother and brother were both there. I remember telling Karen that I wanted to see my mom, if that was possible. It was obvious to me that she could see and hear her, and I wanted to also. Karen responded by saying that my mother had recently come to me in a dream. She was right. Within the past week, preceding the appointment with Karen, I had a lucid dream. A lucid dream is especially vivid, with very bright colors, textures and sometimes fragrances. You feel as if you are actually there participating, not just observing.

In this particular dream I was with my four sisters and we were in a room of some kind. I was standing in front with my four sisters behind me. As I looked in front of me, our mother came out of an area that seemed to be like a dark cave. As she approached I said, "Mom, what are you doing here, you are dead!" She looked at me with her beautiful eyes and said, "Honey, I am not dead, I have just been lost for twenty-seven years." "What... You have been lost?" I turned to my sisters and said, "Can you believe it, she hasn't been dead all this time, she was lost!" We all hugged each other and laughed and cried. Then I woke up.

45

As I relayed this information to Karen, she said, "Your mother wasn't lost, she was talking about you. You have been lost for twenty-seven years." How true that statement was. It had been twenty-seven years since my mother had died. I often felt as though I was just getting through life, not completely sure of what I was meant to do. Since the time of my mother's death in August of 1969 I had always prayed that I would be able to see her someday. Here she was, lovingly letting me know that she had always been with me, and that it was time for me not to be lost anymore. It was true; I had felt lost for a very long time.

In fairly short order, I took some classes that Karen was teaching on intuition development and dream interpretation. I met so many wonderful, talented individuals there. Again, the education continues.

By this time, I was involved with hospice, taking Polarity Therapy classes and learning all that I could about developing my intuition. I had always thought that there was something different about me. There were times as a child that I knew I needed to be alone, that I knew I just needed to think or reflect on things. Gratefully this was a habit that I had developed before my brother and mother's deaths, since the need to reflect on life's events would play a major role in my development as a healer and for my own inner understanding.

We often would have assignments given to us during our Intuition Development class. One such assignment helped to broaden my sense of awareness. You might like to try this yourself. I will describe the technique now and then share with you my own experience.

Sit in a place where you will not be disturbed by the telephone or other people. Have a pad of paper and a pen with you. Sit quietly for fifteen minutes and write down everything that you notice, continually for fifteen minutes. Notice how your body feels, what your clothing feels like, that taste in your mouth, every sound that you hear. Write it all down, every little thing, no matter how insignificant it may appear to be. Keep writing. After fifteen minutes set your paper and pen aside and close your eyes for about ten minutes. Just relax and let your mind be still. Now, when it feels right, open your eyes and see what you notice.

Well, I sat in the great room of my home and wrote continuously for fifteen minutes, often feeling as though I was being redundant by sights, sounds and feelings. I noticed at first this made me feel a bit anxious, but I did it anyway. I wrote down everything. Then when fifteen minutes had passed I set the paper and pen aside and just relaxed. When it felt like it was time to open my eyes, I was astonished by what I saw. From the corner of the room came the most beautiful white dove in flight! Its wings moved without a sound as I sat on the couch in awed silence. In a moment, or two, it faded away.

There was no doubt in my mind that I was blessed with the image of the Holy Spirit. I didn't know what to say or what to think. I just sat there in amazement and wonder. How could this be? Although I had often asked that I would be able to "see" something, I half believed that it would never happen to me. Well, it happened, right in my own family room! Awe does not begin to explain what I was feeling. I felt humbled, struck by the beauty of what I had just seen. I felt as though I had been touched by grace. Then my little mind kicked in. You must have made that up, you were just seeing things. Well, that was correct, I was seeing things!

Believe in yourself

LISTENING

"Let us open up our natures,
throw wide the doors of your hearts
and let in the sunshine
of good will and kindness."

O. S. Marden

Listening to the Angels is not the hardest part. Trusting what you receive, now that is the hard part! Each and every one of us is given messages all of the time, throughout each and every day, but the vast majority of the time we simply do not listen. How many times have you had a nagging feeling to turn right rather than left, and for some inextricable reason that nudge is ignored, and you find yourself locked in a traffic jam? Or have you ever had someone come into your mind, seemingly out of the blue, and a moment later you ran into him or her on the street, or they called you on the phone? Sure, it has happened to each of us.

Those little "whispers" are messages that have been sent to you, and perhaps in a moment of clarity you listened. Then when the message was confirmed, in the call from a friend, you shake your head and wonder how in the world that happened. Never for one moment forget that your thoughts are broadcast out through the ethers, and likewise other people's thoughts are passed through the fabric of time and space.

Then there are times, when the Angels will speak so clearly and precisely to you that you are startled into action. That happened to me in the early morning hours one spring day.

Our son Brian was going on a spring break with some of his friends, but due to a work schedule conflict he did not have the same flight as the rest of the gang. His flight was scheduled for the next morning at 5:30 a.m. which meant that he had to get up very early to get to the airport. He asked me if I could take him, and I readily agreed. He had worked hard and was looking forward to the trip.

So early on the morning of his flight we drove southbound on I-275 going to Detroit Metro Airport. Upon arrival, he got his bags and gave me a hug and kiss goodbye. He promised to let me know when he arrived at his destination safely. Just as I was getting into the car he said, "Mom, please drive safely home, I love you!" "I love you too, darlin'. Have fun!" I said.

As I was getting onto the expressway, I realized that there weren't any other cars on the road, but after all, it was about 4:30 in the morning. It was very dark, as there aren't any streetlights on this particular stretch of road. I was in the far right lane and I realized that I was going faster than the speed limit. All of a sudden, as if someone was in the car with me, I heard, "Do not accelerate, do not brake, do not swerve, stay in your own lane. Everything will be fine." "What the…" I thought. I heard the phrase repeated a few more times. I was a bit confused.

All of a sudden there was a very large raccoon in my lane and I realized that I was going to hit it. The words repeated, "Do not accelerate, do not brake, do not swerve, stay in your own lane. Everything is fine." I was rapidly approaching the raccoon and I felt a momentary relief as it crossed out of my lane and was almost to the middle lane. "Phew," I thought. Then at the last second, he turned back into my lane. "Oh, God, no…please!" then, crunch; I knew that I had killed the raccoon. I felt sick. Then I heard, "Don't be alarmed, you put him out of his misery, he was old, dying and in pain. And, he saved your life."

I was so shaken that I could hardly drive home. I had just killed an animal, I felt sick and… someone was talking to me about it! The scene played over and over in my mind.

The following week, when I went to pick Brian up from the airport we drove home using the exact same route, but this time the sun was shining and I could clearly see what I was guided to avoid. On the right side of the road was a huge hill, that had I not listened, had I panicked, I more than likely would have swerved to avoid hitting the raccoon, and my car surely would have gone down the hill and not have been seen for a very long time. Angels, thank you for protecting me that day. I knew immediately who it was that had spoken to me, and I was extremely grateful.

I could have easily ignored the warning, thinking that I was "just hearing things," and the reality is, I was hearing things! That experience helped to solidify that we are protected when we believe we are not, and even though the Angels may not be heard, they hear us, even when we don't say a word.

GETTING THE MESSAGE

"The one thing grander than the sea is the sky.
The one thing grander than the sky
is the human heart."

Anonymous

The more I worked with clients, the more I began to experience an interesting phenomenon. I began to hear things about the person that I was working with. Before I continue, I would like to explain what I mean by "hearing." God had given us many abilities, our five senses and beyond. Our senses are the foundation of understanding healing, since healing encompasses the totality of our being. And since healing encompasses the entirety of us, then it stands to reason that body, mind and spirit are involved in the healing process, not just that of the person receiving the healing, but the healer too. As a healer, you must learn to employ all of your senses simultaneously in order to fully receive the information that is being given. In other words, you must learn to be present.

How often can you honestly say that you are "present" in any given situation? By being present I mean paying attention to what is occurring right here, right now. The vast majority of our time is spent thinking about what has already occurred or wondering about what might occur. We are not very good at paying attention to the magical moment of "now." That is the only time that is real, everything else is just a memory or a possibility. And most people have pretty faulty memories. Not that they necessarily are fabricating what occurred, but they are remembering through the veil of their emotional experience of the memory, not necessarily remembering what actually occurred. That is why different people can be present at the same "event" yet each has totally different recollection of what occurred.

In the healing process, as I have worked on clients, I would begin to "know" that there were problems that had not been discussed. For instance, while working on a client, my knee might begin to hurt. Knowing that I had not injured my knee, I began to understand that I was feeling what was occurring in my client. I would simply ask that individual what was wrong with their knee. Invariably they would ask how I knew that their knee was hurting. Simply put, their body was attempting to give me information that the client themselves had not shared. Why is this of value?

Think about the many times when you had answered the simple question, "How are you?" and although you might be feeling lousy, your reply might be, "I am fine, thank you." Your body knows that this is not the truth, but many times people do not wish to share, for whatever reason, the entirety of what they are feeling. Unfortunately many times people do not even know what they are feeling themselves, since often they have denied their feelings in order to get through situations. Over time, the ignoring of our own truth will catch up with us.

It is essential for a healer to be "present," thereby allowing yourself to become aware of information that might be useful in assisting a person more completely. The interesting thing is that you may or may not wish to share what you "receive." That is where discretion comes into play. You may not wish to share all that you are intuiting until you have some sense that your client is ready for that information. However, if you detect a problem in the knee, to use the example cited above, you can work on that area of the body to begin to correct an energetic imbalance, thereby eliminating or reducing discomfort. So even though a client may not have mentioned a particular ache or pain, when paying attention, a healer can help to effect a change.

When doing any type of intuitive work one must learn how to not only "hear" but also to "listen." Most people are able to "hear" many things, like outside noises, the sound of footsteps, and the wind in the trees. But how often do you truly "listen" to all that is around you. This quiet concentration allows me to "listen" to the Angels as they guide and support the giving of information. This information could be from a deceased loved one, or it could be information about events that are occurring in the individual's life. The sharing of this information may provide an opportunity for them to look at events, others and themselves with more loving eyes and an open heart.

I was just about to complete my certification as an Associate Polarity Practitioner and had not yet begun to study Healing Touch when I found myself in need of energy healing. I had been home cleaning and needed to move a heavy piece of furniture that had slipped off of the pad that protected the wooden floor. "How hard can this be," I thought, "I could easily slip the small pad under the leg of the sideboard." I lifted it up and heard a "pop" in my back. The next day I could barely move and later discovered that I had ruptured the disk between L5 and S1 of my spinal column. I was in a world of hurt. It even hurt to breathe.

Along with physical therapy I decided that I needed some healing myself, so I went to the Healing Touch Center, a clinic where healers being trained in Healing Touch could work with clients while acquiring the needed experience to complete their certification. One Saturday morning I was in a great deal of pain and

I drove myself to the clinic. As I sat alone in the waiting area, the practitioners were "centering" on the other side of the room dividers.

While I sat waiting, two gentlemen came into the room and joined the others in the centering process. As clear as a bell I heard someone say, "One of those men is going to work on you." Oh really, I thought. Sure enough, as they began to get ready to assign clients with practitioners, a woman named Nancy walked toward me and asked if I would mind if a man worked on me. I didn't mind at all.

A gentleman by the name of Gary came over and sat down with me and began to ask me a few questions. What had brought me here, was I in pain? Within a few moments he became quiet and said, "I don't always do things exactly like everyone else here, is that okay with you?" "Sure," I said, "anything to help reduce this pain." We walked to the area where the healing treatments were done and I laid down on the massage table. Within seconds of lying down I heard, "This man is a priest." Interesting, I thought.

Within a very short time, I realized that Gary had some extraordinary gifts. Almost immediately, I felt as though I had a kaleidoscope of colors and sensations going through my body. Before he even touched me I could sense mild jolts of electricity running through me. Every now and then Gary would say, "That's cool," and "Hum, never saw that before." Before long, it was time to get off the table.

A typical healing treatment at the clinic lasts for one hour from the time that you begin to intake information from the client until the time you have them off the table and are evaluating what has occurred. Well, Gary and I spent two and a half hours together that day. Not typical, to say the least. As we sat facing one other

I asked him if he was a priest. He laughed and said, "They told me you were good." Puzzled, I asked again if he was a priest. No, he said, but he had been in the seminary. There was no doubt in my mind that this was a holy man, one full of good humor and compassion. But who, I wondered, had been talking to him about me?

Gary then did something that I will never forget. He took both of my hands in his, looked me straight in the eyes and said, "You know you are a healer, don't you?" "Well," I stammered, "I am finishing up my training in Polarity Therapy." He then said, "No, you know you are a healer, don't you?" I reluctantly said yes and then shared that I had been a bit afraid to do it, not sure that I wanted the responsibility and wondering why I was being given so much information about people. He just looked at me and told me that he had a few people that he wanted me to meet.

Then, while still holding my hands, he put his head down slightly and said, "I need to tell you something so that you aren't frightened when it happens. At least three times, and probably more, you will be working with people that are given a terminal diagnosis and they will be completely cured." I immediately withdrew my hands from his and said, "You have got the wrong person!" His next words were, "God doesn't make mistakes." To say that I was a little shaken would be an understatement. Who was telling him this stuff, I thought incredulously. Soon I would learn that it was the Angels and other Beings of Light.

Gary told me that he wanted me to meet two people, Katherine and Bill. He told me that Katherine was in her eighties and that she was a gifted intuitive. He gave me her card and told me where she lived and I realized that it was very near where I had to be on the following Monday. Perhaps I could arrange to meet her then.

He then told me about the other intuitive that he wanted me to meet. "Bill is an unusual character, in fact, he can be quite intimidating," Gary said. The man he wanted me to meet was a retired foreman of a manufacturing plant, and Gary added, not someone who usually likes to meet new people. "Why then, would you want me to meet him?" I asked. "I am being told that you have to," he replied. Ok then. Gary also told me of a shrine not too far from where Katherine lived. "It's a pretty cool place, you should go there sometime." What do I have to lose? It sounded interesting, and I thought that perhaps I would check it out someday.

I sat for a few minutes in my car, feeling a bit dazed. What was all of that about, I wondered. While driving home from the clinic I had a rather bossy conversation with God. I was the one being bossy. "If you want me to do this work then you had better bring the clients to me, because I am not going to look for them. Besides, I am not sure what to do other than what I am doing. But, if you send them, I promise that I will do the healing work." After all, God is the healing force anyway, and He knows who is in need of assistance far better than I ever could. Well, remember that asking will produce results. It did, quicker than I could have imagined.

Within an hour of returning home I received a call from my life-long friend, Kim. Kim and I have known each other since first grade so to say that we know each other well is an understatement. She told me that her brother-in-law Robert had been to the doctor's office just the day before getting a routine physical. His physician told him, "Robert you are going to live to be a hundred. You are as healthy as a horse." But Robert told his doctor that he had been feeling more tired than usual and requested that he do some blood work. The physician agreed and having done that sent Robert home.

Later that day the telephone rang. It was the hospital. The man on the line told Robert that there was a problem with his blood and that he needed to get to the hospital immediately. Several times Robert asked what was wrong. Finally, the man told him that he had leukemia. Stunned, Robert asked him what that meant. The man said that he had maybe two weeks to live.

Kim told me that Robert was in the hospital. Then I told her about the events of that day in the clinic. "Kim, if Robert and Gail are interested, I would be happy to go to the hospital to work with Robert. Would you want to call Gail and ask what they think?" She said she would call them right away.

Gail called me a few minutes later. I told her that I didn't know to what extent it could help but I was willing to try if Robert wanted me to come. He was scheduled to be in the hospital for a month, undergoing intense chemotherapy while still reeling from the shock of this news. We made arrangements for me to begin doing healing work with him the following day.

Robert is an extraordinary man, a gifted artist, a beloved teacher, author, and one who was being given the opportunity to begin to heal and regain his health. I was given the gift of believing that it was okay for me to be a healer and to trust what God had in mind for me. We both were blessed that day. Here is Robert's experience in his own words.

"You will live to be a hundred," Dr. H said after giving me a complete exam on the morning of April 14, 2000... and I think he really meant it.

Heart, blood pressure, etc. all checked out fine, and I left feeling on top of the world. At four o'clock that afternoon he called to tell me that some of the blood work came back and that I should

58

get into a hospital for further tests. At first, he was hesitant to reveal his suspicions, but when pressed said it might be leukemia. When pressed further, for a worse case scenario, he told me that I had two weeks to live. Instantly, the world I was feeling on top of fell completely apart.

Hanging up the phone, I realized that I was alone in the house, that I had cancer and that I could die. Hours later, I asked the doctor in the emergency room if it was true or not that I had two weeks to live, "Well maybe," he replied, "you could have three." Two days later, at the age of fifty-eight, the bone marrow test results confirmed that I had Acute Mylogenic Leukemia.

It's been over nine years now since cancer visited my body. I'm still alive, and doing remarkably well, although I don't totally understand why. I can, however, tell you how one person may have made the life saving difference.

My wife's sister had a good friend named Elaine Grohman. As it turned out, I had met Elaine on several occasions over the years, but I honestly didn't know her. However, within the first couple of days after I first discovered my illness, she asked if she could come to the hospital to do energy work on me. These were difficult if not confusing days, and not knowing much about energy work, I took comfort in her kindness and said yes.

Elaine immediately started coming to the hospital. Several times a week she would spend an hour working on me. As first I wasn't sure of how this unseen energy force was affecting me, or how I was to welcome it, but as we began to recognize each other's spiritual dimensions I became more and more grateful for each visit.

There isn't much in the world that isn't caused by things unseen. This includes cancer as well as the healing of cancer. Working with unseen energies, Elaine somehow began activating both my body and my spirit into responding to the energy each session attracted. Gradually I gained an awareness of energy forces within me. They became a new part of my reality in the way that possessions were part of my physical reality. With Elaine, I was able to experience the flowing of life energy through my being. After each session I would feel as if I had gently crossed over some barrier into some place of personal peace.

I think where the healing came in was through the feelings of freedom that lasted for many hours following each session. These were states of relaxation where my energies were harmonious and I was able to assume the universal energies of my spirit and move beyond the distressing fears of my physical circumstances. I already knew that our spirits were not of the physical domain, but what I needed to know was that my spirit and not my body had to become my primary reality. I needed the space to trust the reality of my spirit as much as the reality of medicine.

Now, I know who Elaine is. Now, she is my respected friend and dare I say it, angel. She will always have my ever-present gratitude, for without her continuous presence, wisdom and positive support I might not have been able to step far enough away from the paralyzing fears that cancer were presenting me with. To this day, I still look forward to my energy treatments with her and to coming into closer contact with her gifts and those higher energies that have become part of my life force and spiritual strength."

Robert Piepenburg

THE ANGELS AND ME

THE BREATH OF AN ANGEL

*"Hold out your hands
to feel the luxury of the sunbeams."*

Helen Keller

That same Saturday afternoon, still amazed by the whole experience, I decided to put in a call to Katherine, the elderly woman Gary had spoken of. I left a message on her answering machine that I would be in her area on Monday, asking if there was any possibility of meeting her? On Sunday I received a return phone call and was delighted to hear her Irish brogue as she agreed to meet with me on Monday afternoon. What a weekend that had been!

The room in which Katherine worked was like walking into a Catholic bookstore. Statues, paintings and religious artifacts were everywhere, nestled among her many family photos. This was a holy woman, one who had taken a great deal of criticism over the years, but as a devout Catholic knew enough to trust God, and not to necessarily listen to the fears and dogma of others. She helped countless people with her loving ability to give Divine messages. She read my palms and gave me very precise information about my life, something that she could not possibly have known.

She repeated what Gary had said to me two days before, "I am being told that you are a healer. You know you are a healer, don't you?" "Who is saying that to you?" I asked. She simply smiled and said, "My friend." "Who is your friend?" I asked. "Jesus is my friend. He and his mother talk to me all the time, and both are here with us now, telling me to tell you not to be afraid." Holy cow, now Jesus and Mary were talking to people…about me! I was not only afraid… I was petrified!

After the reading I decided to see if I could find the shrine that Gary had mentioned. I found it without too much trouble. As I pulled into the lot behind the small building I noticed that I had accidentally pulled into the handicapped parking space, so I backed up into another spot with the front of my car facing the shrine and the parking lot. As I walked into the building I was amazed at what I saw. It was full of every kind of religious statue, crucifixes, rosaries, candles…every kind of religious symbol that you can imagine. There were letters tacked onto the walls giving thanks for the blessed events that had occurred there, along with folded wheelchairs, crutches, canes and other artifacts that indicated that many extraordinary things had taken place here.

I was alone when suddenly a little nun came into the room. She had a very heavy accent and asked me if I would like her to pray with me. I thanked her and said yes. She started to pray in her native language and when she was done she quietly left. As I walked around looking at the fully packed room, a little old man walked in. I decided to leave to give him the opportunity to be alone in this place.

I walked out and sat in my car, thinking about the strange events that happened in the last few days. I noticed a car as it pulled into the parking lot and a gentleman got out of his car and crossed in front of me. I was startled as I realized that I recognized this man. It was Gary! I got out and called his name. He laughed and got into my car. The likelihood of this happening astonished both of us. Gary's home was well over an hour's drive away and here he was walking into the building that I had just come out of. We sat together in my car as he explained that he was on his way to visit his buddy Bill. He decided to stop at the shrine before going on to Bill's home. I asked if he thought it might be okay if I went with him. He put in a call to Bill, whose answer was, no, not today. Gary reiterated that Bill was a very private man and didn't like to have strangers at his house. Perhaps some other time. That was fine with me, I wasn't sure I could take any more surprises.

Two days later I went back to the Healing Touch Center and again Gary was there. He took me aside and said, "Well, Bill wanted to know when he could meet that woman I had been talking about." He meant me. How about today, I said. He called Bill and before long we were in the car driving to Bill's house.

While driving to Bill's home, Gary shared information about their unique relationship and warned me that I was about to meet a very tough cookie. I had known a tough cookie all of my life. We arrived at the modest home of Bill and his wife Dolores. Answering the door, Bill looked every bit the picture of the tough guy that Gary had described. His wife, on the other hand, was gregarious and bubbly. They invited us in and led us to the lower level of their tri-level home.

Walking down the stairs I was amazed at what I saw. There were about one hundred model airplanes of all shapes and sizes hanging from the ceiling. There were so many planes that I was sure that their wings might touch if there was any wind. Many paintings surrounded the room, stacked against one another, others displayed on the walls. Bill was an artist, and a very accomplished one at that. He had been a World War II pilot and that time in his history was depicted everywhere.

I commented on the volume and the intricacy of his work and mentioned that my brother Brian had been an excellent model builder. This flooded me with memories of my sweet brother. Unceremoniously, Bill pointed to four chairs and told me to sit down. Bill was to my right, Dolores to my left and Gary directly across from me. Within minutes, Bill began to relay an amazing story to me. He and his wife were the parents of nine children. Bill had been a foreman at a large manufacturing plant when a terrible accident occurred on the floor of the plant. Bill was not expected to live. As he struggled to remain conscious he suddenly was aware of the fact that he was not in the plant, but was standing in a large room. He was out of his body.

As he stood there wondering where he was, others began to enter the room. Slowly he recognized them. They were fellow soldiers from the war. Each had lost their lives in the battles there. Something wasn't right, he realized. If he was seeing all of these men then that meant that he must be dead. There was no way that he was going to leave his wife alone with nine kids. Another figure entered the room. Gradually, Bill realized that it was Jesus himself. Amazed by what he was seeing, Bill reached out to touch Him. Without saying a word, Jesus withdrew, out of Bill's reach. I sat in amazement as he continued his recollection. Bill said that the beautiful garment Jesus was wearing mesmerized him, and he desperately wanted to touch it. "If you touch me, Bill, you have to stay here." Well, Bill did not want to stay, but being a foreman he was used to telling people what he wanted done.

Before long, Jesus gave him permission to touch him, and the moment he did, Bill felt the crushing pain of his injuries as he realized he was back in his body. Bill continued as I sat in stunned silence. Since that time, he told me, Jesus had been a constant companion, and with Bill being able to see him with his eyes wide open. Not only that, but Bill began to realize that he had the ability to heal and was often told where to place his hands in order to help others. Holy smokes, I thought, as he continued with his amazing story.

A few years after Bill's near fatal accident and his long recuperation, his beloved Dolores developed breast cancer. By this time Bill had developed the unique ability to know if someone had something wrong, often before the doctors knew. This gift is called being a medical intuitive. Dolores was scheduled to have surgery. As he and one of his children waited for Dolores's surgery to be complete, a woman was being rolled past them on the way to the recovery room. His son said that it was his mother, while Bill didn't seem to recognize her. As the gurney rolled by all Bill could see was a grey cloud covering the person on the gurney. Well, it was his wife, and he and his son were brought to the recovery room. With Bill's abilities he realized that something was terribly wrong. Immediately he called upon Jesus to help him.

Bill stated that standing on the opposite side of the gurney in the recovery room was Jesus. "Do something!" Bill demanded. He said that Jesus simply looked at him and said, "No Bill, you do something!" Well, Bill lost his temper a little bit and said, "You are Jesus, not me, heal her!" Can you imagine that? Calmly Jesus told Bill to put his hand on Dolores, as she lay there very ashen. So Bill did what he was told, and he immediately noticed that her complexion was pinking up. Pink, pink, pink. All of a sudden she opened her eyes and said, "Hi honey, I am so thirsty, can I have something to drink?" No grogginess, no pain, no nothing, just his sweet wife lying there as if nothing had happened. She never needed any pain medication and felt completely fine. Her doctors were amazed.

Jiminy Crickets, what was I supposed to say to that? I just sat there in amazement. The next thing I knew Bill was looking at me, or rather looking beyond me. What the heck is he doing, I thought. Then he looked straight at me and said, "Young lady, you know you are a healer, don't you?" Oh boy, here we go again! "I suppose so," I said. He repeated, more firmly this time, "You know you are a healer, don't you?" "How do you know that?" I demanded. Calmly, he stated that the man behind me was telling him that. "Who is standing behind me," I asked, a bit shaken. Bill told me that Jesus was standing behind me and was telling him so, that was how he knew. I felt sick and tingly all at the same time.

"You know why you are here, don't you?" he asked me. I said that Gary had thought that I should meet him, and after all, he had said that I could come over. "Not here in this house, here in this life!" "You are a healer, and you are here to help to change medicine." My head was spinning. "And I would like you to work on my wife Dolores. I have only allowed a few people to work on her, of which Gary and his brother were two, besides myself." I looked to my left and asked Dolores, "Is it alright with you if I work on you?" "Sure," she said with a smile.

We made arrangements for me to come back the following week to begin to do healing work with her. Over the next several months I visited and continued to do healing treatments with her. Each time I arrived I knew that Bill was watching my every move. Over time, his rough exterior began to soften as he shared tours of his small studio space and even did a healing on me.

The first time that I did healing work with Dolores, an amazing thing happened. The moment I put my hands on her, one small yellow bi-plane began to move back and forth very slowly. This little plane was completely surrounded by other model planes, which stayed perfectly still, with their wings having barely enough room between them. There was no vent at the ceiling level and nothing that was causing the small plane to move. It just did. When that happened both Dolores and I saw it move in a slow rhythmic way. "Your brother is here, you know" she said sweetly. I smiled at the thought of Brian playing with the model plane. As soon as I completed the treatment with Dolores, the little yellow bi-plane stopped moving. Thanks for the support, Brian. I love you too. This happened each time I worked with Dolores.

I was not completely sure what to do with all of the experiences I was having. If someone else had told me all of these things were happening to them I might have questioned the validity of what they said, or at least their sanity. But, Jiminy Crickets, all of this was happening to me! Sometimes it made me tired just thinking of it all. All I knew was that God was in charge. So every morning as I awake I simply ask, "Make me an instrument of your peace." After all, healing is where peace resides. Chaos is where illness thrives. And I would find that illness comes in many forms, from a sick body to an angry heart. All of this was helping me to be prepared for the work that I was about to begin.

The profoundest
changes in
life are made
in the
human heart.

Going Beyond Our Boundaries

"Treasure this day, and treasure yourself.
Truly, neither will ever happen again."

Ray Bradbury

Over time, as I worked with clients, I began to "hear" or perhaps "know" that there was a problem that the client had neglected to mention before a treatment. This information would become palpable to me in the form of pain in my own body. For instance, if a client had a problem with their knee, I might experience pain in my knee or I might feel the pain in my hand as I touched the client's knee. Emotional pain would also become evident and at first, I must admit, I was not sure what to make of it. Finally, I would simply ask my client if they had a problem in that particular area or if something was bothering them.

Time, and time again, their answer would be "yes, how did you know that?" I began to trust that their body was giving me information in order to help the healing process. It did not take too long to understand the significance of these events. Now think about this for a moment. How many times have you been to a health care provider and did not tell them about all of the pain that you were experiencing. This does not mean that you were necessarily avoiding or withholding information intentionally, although that might be the case. More than likely, you had gone in for another reason, let's say a sore throat, so that was the primary focus of your appointment. You might have had a problem with the knee but that was out of your thoughts at the moment. Or, another possibility could be that you did not want to appear to be a complainer, so you selected what you thought should be shared.

You can imagine how many times this occurs when people are seeking assistance with a medical, emotional or spiritual problem. Perhaps we are taught to handle only one problem at a time. But consider how ignoring a problem can start an entire chain of events. When one system has a problem other systems have to compensate.

Let's take for instance, if you had a sore back. You might hold yourself differently as you walk, sit or stand. This in turn puts stress on other parts of the body as you try to find some comfort. Couple that with the pain that may prevent you from thinking clearly or allow you to have a restful sleep. This snowball effect can set up a chain of events that effect the entire person, body, mind and spirit.

As an energy worker I was directed to pay attention to other areas of the body that were in need of healing. Sometimes the pain would be emotional. Sometimes there was a sense of grief, sadness or anger that became palpable. Believe me, I was puzzled as to why all of this was occurring. I later learned that this was a gift that I had the opportunity to hone so that I could be a more affective and empathetic healer. If a practitioner is paying attention, they may begin to start a dialogue with the client to help them view their life's events with a fresh eye. This sets the stage for forgiveness. Sometimes the greatest pain that affects someone is not always physical pain, but rather spiritual or emotional pain.

Let's say for instance that someone had been angry over an event in his or her earlier life. Unresolved anger creates a veil by which we view the world and every moment of that life is seen through the veil of that emotion. Unfortunately, that often prevents us from seeing or knowing what is really occurring. Acknowledging a past fear or anger does not make the event all right, rather it helps the individual see that they have the opportunity to learn about themselves in relation to any event. Then, from that perspective they can begin to see the truth about what occurred. Love is the healing force that brings peace and comfort to us all. I was being given the tools to help to bring that Force to the foreground. By helping others, I have been able to help myself. But first, I needed to learn to pay close attention, and to trust the information that I was being given. Circumstances present themselves to help us learn to trust.

There was an event that helped me to begin to see how helpful our intuition could be for another's healing and self -awareness. I was working at the healing clinic and as the practitioners waited to be assigned a client, I noticed one woman who sat waiting for a treatment. I remember noticing her body language and thinking, oh boy, whoever has to work with her will really have a challenge.

Within a few minutes, I was asked if I would work with her. Before any healing work begins, a short conversation takes place between the client and the practitioner. The intention is to glean information regarding the purpose of the visit. Questions are asked to determine if the client is in pain, and if so, to rate it on a scale of 0-10; 10 being the worst. This information is a tool to gauge the effectiveness of the treatment. When the treatment is complete another assessment is done. The practitioner may ask other questions to begin to understand the impact that their pain is having on their life. This, along with other information, is used to guide the practitioner.

While doing the intake interview, I noticed that her body language was very closed. Her legs crossed, arms folded across her chest, head lowered and speaking with short clipped words. I asked her why she had chosen to come, as it appeared that she clearly did not wish to be there. "My husband made me come," was her reply. She continued to tell me that she was in a great deal of pain, and that this pain was impacting her ability to do her job. She had struggled with this discomfort for some time, having undergone many medical interventions along with some surgical procedures. Nothing helped to reduce her pain. She was unable to rotate her arm without terrible pain in her shoulder. This was not acceptable to her and her husband was trying anything to help her feel better.

Several times I asked her what her job was and she was reluctant to reply. Finally, she answered. "I am an emergency room physician." Oh boy, this might be a challenge, I thought. As I had been having more and more intuitive experiences I typically ask the client if I may share any intuitive information that I might receive. The answer was "yes." She rated her pain at a nine. This is significant pain, I thought.

My client and I walked to the treatment area and we prepared to begin. I stood to the side of the massage table and the moment I touched her I saw an entire scene play out in my mind's eye. I began to view an emergency room, complete with all the medical equipment, staff and patients. All of a sudden, I witnessed my client yelling at everyone, and it was as though I was seeing it through her eyes. She was barking orders with anger in her words. In a moment, I began to see her from the perspective of the people she was yelling at. It seemed as though I could read their thoughts. Immediately I got the impression that she was highly regarded as a technician, but her personality left people in shock. I opened my eyes and said, "May I be frank with you?"

"Yes," she replied. I took a deep breath and asked the Angels to help me say these words so that they would be heard. "Why are you yelling at people in the emergency room? You are being given an opportunity here. There are medical residents that are learning from you and you have an opportunity to teach them how to be competent, angry physicians or you can teach them how to be competent, compassionate physicians. You have a choice here. You are a fabulous technician, but you need to bring love to this chaos." She opened her eyes and with a surprised look on her face she asked, "How did you know that I taught residents in the ER?" All I could say was that I had seen it. I was grateful that I was learning to trust the Angels. The information that I was given was accurate and important.

The treatment continued. I asked her about the pain in her knee, then her opposite hip, and other places in her body. "How do you know that?" was her constant question. "Your body is telling me," was my reply. Finally the treatment ended and we sat together to talk about what had just occurred. I asked her to reassess her pain level and she stated that it was at zero. "How could that be? I have missed my pain meds and I don't feel any pain right now. Are you psychic or something?" she asked. I told her my belief is that we are all intuitive, that it is an innately human ability, it is just that some of us are beginning to trust that ability to use it to help others.

Before leaving the clinic, she asked me if she could have my home number, in case she had any questions. A few days later I received a phone call from her. "This is Dr. G., do you remember me?" How could I forget? "I have a question. What the hell did you do to me?" I was shocked and replied, "In relation to what?" "I told you that I had been in a great deal of pain, and that I had pathology in that shoulder." "Yes, I recall," I said. "After leaving the clinic, I was overdue for my pain medication and I was not in pain. In fact, I had no pain whatsoever for hours, and that has not happened for over two years. What the hell did you do?"

Okay God, I thought, give me a really good explanation so that this ER physician can understand what occurred. "Okay, imagine that you have a patient that comes into the emergency room and they have a broken arm. What would your job be at that point?" I didn't give her the opportunity to answer. Continuing I said, "You would need to x-ray the arm and then set those bones, correct?" Yes, that was correct. "Once those bones were set into their proper alignment and then put in a cast, would you follow that person home to continue the healing?" "No, of course not," was her answer. "No, you just put those bones in place so that your patient's body could begin to heal, right? Well, all I did was set your energetic bones, so that your body could heal itself." She thought for a moment and then said that that explanation made perfect sense to her. Phew, thanks God, for that one.

Before ending the conversation she asked if she could come to see me in my home. We made arrangement for her to come to have a treatment the following week. The second time we worked together, she was willing to share her own personal experiences of being an intuitive. As a child she had been able to see and know when something was about to happen to someone, or when something had happened and her family had not known yet. She knew what a child would not have known. This frightened her mother who told her that this kind of information would only come from something evil and that she had to stop it. She continued to see and know things, but did not feel safe to share that information. Over time, she began to shut down her intuitive gifts.

As she began her medical education and residency she met a senior physician who would become a mentor. This other physician was a gifted healer, having been raised in a culture that honored the gift that she had. The elder physician was aware of this gift in Dr. G., although she herself has avoided it for years. As they worked together in the hospital she would be asked to observe a patient to see if she could intuit what was the real problem. More times than not, she was correct.

After her second treatment, she again called me and told me that this time she had no pain for several days after the treatment. "That is a good thing, don't you think?" I said. She came one more time and I have not heard from her again. I sincerely hope that she has begun to use her gifts of healing and insight to become the physician that she was meant to be. After all, the Hippocratic oath states, "First, do no harm."

I was fortunate enough to have many experiences like this that helped me to listen. Listening and trusting would help me to help others in ways that I could never do alone.

THE SEEN AND THE UNSEEN

"Truth has no special time of its own.
Its hour is now – always."

Albert Schweitzer

Many times I had prayed, hoping that my prayers were heard, but truly I was not sure if they were. Then one day, those doubts began to evaporate. I had had several intuitive readings over the years, and each time the individual would give me very similar information. They all said, "You could do exactly what I am doing if you wanted to." I wasn't sure that I wanted to have that gift, or for that matter, that responsibility.

In late December 2001, a client told me of a young, gifted psychic by the name of Rebecca Rosen . She shared her experience with me and suggested that I might want to make an appointment with her. Intrigued, I called and took her first available date - February 28, 2002. I marked the date and time on my calendar and put it out of my mind.

Behind the scenes of life, mysterious circumstances were playing out which would bring validation to the work that I was doing in a startling way and help me to understand, deep in my heart, that our actions, thoughts and words never go unnoticed.

On February 10, 2002 my friend Bonnie Topper, an incredibly dedicated hospice nurse, called to ask me if I could see one of her patients, a young wife and mother who was dying of a brain tumor. Her patient's husband was doing everything he could to make his wife as comfortable as possible, knowing that her life was rapidly coming to an end. Bonnie suggested that perhaps some energy healing would be helpful. I spoke with her husband and we made arrangements for me to come to their home the following day. His wife's name was Gayle.

I saw her three times in a ten day period. The first and last time, she was completely comatose, chemically sedated in an attempt to manage her pain. The middle time she was having some physical care done, and she was clearly aware that I was with her, and although it was difficult she could communicate with me. Each and every time I worked with her, I silently prayed, asking the Archangels Michael, Gabriel, Raphael and Uriel to stand around her bed. I knew in my heart that they would be able to help her with her pain and help her to release from her body when it was time. She passed away quietly on February 22, 2002, with her husband lovingly by her side. Six days later, on February 28, 2002 I had my scheduled appointment with the young medium, Rebecca Rosen.

The Universe has the uncanny ability to weave the fabric of events long before the event arrives. Like the weaver, who may have an idea in her mind, selects the perfect threads and then begins, slowly and intentionally, to bring the threads together to create beauty that is visible. But all along, this magnificent tapestry consists of simple individual strands, individual events, that when brought together make the whole.

Six days after Gayle's death, I walked into Rebecca's office and met a fellow traveler on the beautiful road that opens our hearts and lives to the wonder of all that silently surrounds us. As we met for the first time there was a sense of recognition, as if we were seeing a friend again after a long time had passed.

"There are so many Angels around you!" she said as we sat in her comfortable office. She began to give me messages about the work I was doing and I was repeatedly covered from head to toe with chills, each confirming the information that she provided. She knew my life without having known me. Then, about halfway through the reading, she simply looked above my head and said, "There is a woman here who wants your attention in the worst way. She is saying that she was not a family member or a friend. She was a client of yours, you did some kind of healing work with her."

Having been involved with several hospice patients I was not immediately sure to whom she was referring. Then she said, "Her death was around the corner, and she had cancer. She is saying that the predominate sounds of her name are A and L." "Oh my goodness, is it Gayle?" I asked. Rebecca continued, "She wants to thank you for the healing work that you did because you removed her pain, but most importantly, she wants to thank you for sending the Angels to stand next to her bed." I was dumbstruck… they were listening, and they came to comfort her as she lay dying. Tears rolled down my face. I couldn't continue to believe that these confirmations were mere coincidences. They were far greater, and I was only just beginning to comprehend that.

I was so intrigued by the accuracy of the messages I received that day that I knew I had to learn who it was that had been talking to me and how I might begin to learn to discern who it was, what they wanted me to know, and why they were working with me. Within a few weeks, I was given yet another confirmation when I received an unsolicited email from Rebecca that had an attached article that explained how she began to develop her skills. It felt directed at me, since it answered the question that had been racing through my mind since the reading.

How could I learn to do that? I wanted to know who was helping me but had no idea where to start. In the article, Rebecca shared her experiences of studying with Doreen Virtue, PhD , the well-known author and gifted medium whose work with the Angels is chronicled on many bookstore shelves.

Perhaps I was meant to help others by giving messages to them from an unseen source. I had already been working for years as an Energy Healer and in that time had received many messages from "somewhere" but was not always willing to share that information with my clients. Within a few months of my reading with Rebecca I was studying with Doreen Virtue, Ph.D., and learning what it meant to do Angel Readings. The experiences of that week opened not only my eyes and heart, but released wounds that I thought had healed long before.

Simplicity of the heart is far from being simple.

THE RELEASEMENT

"It has been released."

Archangel Gabriel

Trust is a funny thing. Sometimes you have it, sometimes you don't. But the moment that you know that trust is required of you in an unmistakable way, it can shake you to your core. The workshop with Doreen Virtue, Ph.D. entitled "Angel Therapy" took place in Chicago in August 2002. After my experience with Rebecca Rosen and the visit from my former client, there was nothing that would stop me from learning more about these incredible experiences that I was having. Why were Angelic Beings responding to me? Sure, we are taught that the angels exist and that we can pray to them but never in my wildest dreams did I ever imagine that my prayers would be answered, and especially acknowledged by a deceased woman six days after her death.

I shared this experience with my friend Lenore, who immediately said that she would like to join me. I loved the thought of having her company. Before long we were on our way. We arrived at the hotel and laughed as we discovered that we had brought many of the same things. Candles, music, and books... we definitely thought alike. Each morning before the busy day of the workshop, we would meditate and ask that we be clear in our intentions to learn as much as we could, wishing to be open, willing to explore and have fun. We met some fantastic people that week, some of whom I hope will remain lifelong friends.

The format of the each day's workshop allowed us to open the "clairs:" clairvoyance or clear sight, claircognizance or clear knowing, clairaudience or clear hearing, and clairsentient or clear feeling. Each of these are important ways in which information is shared and received. As we began to acknowledge and trust what was occurring, amazing things began to happen.

In that week we learned how to discern various energies: an Angel vs. a Guide; a deceased loved one vs. the information about someone living; as well as clarity about a person's life events or personal beliefs that might be hindering their ability to live a more loving, joyful life. We learned how to use the totality of our senses to receive information, and then how to interpret the meaning of a message, with an open, truthful and peaceful heart.

The fourth day of the workshop, Steven Farmer, Doreen Virtue's husband and co-presenter, was preparing us for the last evening's sacred ceremony called The "Releasement" Ceremony. The intention of the ceremony was for each of us to acknowledge whatever we needed to release from our minds and hearts so that we would be able to open our hearts and move forward in our lives. These could be experiences, fears or grief, anything that was no longer serving us. We were given the following instructions: to gather a natural object, and before going to bed that evening we were to write down on a piece of paper all of the things we wished to have released. We were to then place the paper on the nightstand and then place the natural object on the sheet of paper containing our list. Before falling asleep, we would ask the Angels and the Nature Spirits to help us to release our worries during the night.

Thursday at lunchtime a group of us went out to a nearby restaurant. On the way to eat, we passed a long hedge. I remember looking at the bush and it seemed as though one little leaf was screaming for my attention. This little green leaf was exactly the same as all the others on the plant, but one in particular caught my eye. So I asked its permission to pick it off of the branch, and I placed it in my pocket. Almost immediately I had second thoughts. This little leaf could never possibly handle all of the things that I wished to release, I thought. So, as a precaution, I picked up two rocks. I know this may sound silly, but I felt as though the little leaf objected to the second choices, so when I arrived back at the hotel, I put the rocks back on the ground. Later that night, Lenore and I sat on our beds and wrote our lists. We dutifully placed the folded paper on the nightstand with the natural object on each list.

A strange thing happened that night as we lay in our beds in the darken room talking into the wee hours of the night. At one point, Lenore quietly said, "Elaine, do you notice anything funny about the ceiling?" As I continued to stare at the ceiling, I realized that the ceiling wasn't there. I was looking up at what appeared to be a beautiful night sky full of stars. I said, "Do you mean the fact that it's not there? Do you see the stars too?" It seemed at first to be the most natural thing in the world. Then we realized that it wasn't possible for us to be lying under the stars, since there were several more floors above our hotel room. We laid there in awe as we softly whispered to each other our amazement. Slowly the night sky faded and the white ceiling came back into our view. There was nothing either of us could say except, "Good Night, my friend."

Before leaving our room the next morning, we decided to put our papers and natural objects in paper cups and place them on the top shelf of the closet, ensuring that the housekeeping staff would not discard them when cleaning the room. We arrived for the daily yoga meditation before starting the day's adventures and eagerly waited what the day would bring. The morning was very interesting as we each had the opportunity to work in our small groups and discover more about the incredible ways in which Divine Guidance is given. Some of the assistants at the workshop offered to give Angel Readings and I made arrangements to have a reading with a wonderful woman named Margaret.

The "Releasement Ceremony" was to be conducted by Steven Farmer that evening at 7:00 p.m. I had made an arrangement to have a reading at 6:00 pm with Margaret. My friend Lenore offered to go to our room to get our cups and then grab a salad for each of us at a deli down the street. That way I would be able to have my scheduled reading and we would each have a chance to get a bite to eat before the evening's activities. My reading was delayed until 6:30 so Lenore and I sat down to eat.

Lenore looked puzzled and she said to me, "Elaine, the weirdest thing happened when I was walking to the deli to get our dinner. I had gone up to the room to get the cups containing our paper and natural object. I was walking down the street carrying a cup in each hand. The weird thing was that your cup was getting so hot that I could hardly hold it! Believe it or not, I had to ask for a paper bag to put it in because it was too hot to hold. I have no idea what is going on!"

We sat down to eat, and I put my little cup immediately next to a large cup of iced tea. Margaret was ready to do the reading with me so I asked Lenore to keep an eye on my food. As I walked towards Margaret I distinctly heard, "It has been released." I remember turning around to see who had just spoken to me. No one was there. So I sat with Margaret and she asked me to close my eyes to begin to meditate and before I knew it I had the sensation that I was floating out of my body. As I sat with my eyes closed I felt incredibly relaxed.

Then I noticed that I heard Margaret begin to cry. Keeping my eyes closed, I asked her if she was all right. "Yes," she said, "I am crying because Archangel Gabriel is here with a message for you. She wants me to tell you that it has been released." Still in a deep meditative state, I told her what had just happened moments before. We both cried as she continued to share the beautiful messages. When our time was up, we hugged each other and I thanked Margaret for this wonderful experience and for her gift.

As I slowly walked back to the table where Lenore was sitting I noticed that my little cup containing my list and the small leaf were gone. I couldn't find it anywhere. Lenore assured me that no one had been there, since she had been sitting there eating the entire time. The salad and the cup of iced tea was still where I had left it. Suddenly I remembered the words that I had heard as a walked over to the reading. "It has been released." At that moment I realized that I didn't need to wait for a Releasement Ceremony, a Divine Being, Archangel Gabriel, had already done that for me. I was humbled and grateful.

I wasn't sure what I was supposed to do after that. Within a matter of minutes the Ceremony was scheduled to begin. I walked up to Steven Farmer and told him what happened. He simply looked at me, smiled, and said, "You have just been given a blessing."

We had been asked to bring some type of rattle or noisemaker to the Releasement Ceremony. I had nothing to bring but myself. As the evening's activity began, I decided that I would just stand in the circle and sing... that's right, sing.

I had recently purchased a wonderful CD by a Native American by the name of John Two Hawks. I had heard this wonderful musician while working with a client, who I had the privilege of being with when she passed away. John Two Hawks songs seemed so appropriate even though some of the words were in the Lakota language. There was one particular song that I knew I had to sing as I stood in that sacred circle that evening in Chicago. I could stand in the circle and sing support to my fellow participants who were about to release their heartaches. How could you do anything else but support such an event?

It was a moving experience. The last portion of the event was to take place just outside of the conference room. It was a lovely evening, and as the most important event was about to occur, a very large boat began to pull up to the dock. Steven Farmer simply asked the people on the boat if they would consider giving us a little more time. This seemingly simple request was really remarkable since this large boat, with over fifty people onboard, was on a very tight cruise schedule. They gracefully agreed to take a little extra spin on the river so that our sacred ceremony could conclude. We were all grateful to the boatload of lawyers, and they were able to party a little longer than they had anticipated.

Wonderful friends were made that week. Lessons were learned. Trust was built. Not only between human friends but also between my human heart and the Divine world.

THE ANGELS AND ME

THE ANGELS AND ME

Learning to Trust

"My wish for you is that the spirit of beauty
may continually hover about you
and fold you close
within the tenderness of her wings."

Charles Snell

Having completed the requirements for certification as an Angel Therapy Practitioner, I began to do readings for people in my home. People allowed me to work with them and soon I began to get referrals from clients.

I recall one woman who came to see me to have a reading. Her demeanor was closed, as she was not willing to offer the slightest clue as to why she was there. All of a sudden I began to hear a name repeating over and over again in my mind. "Rachel, Rachel, Rachel." But that didn't seem quite right. I couldn't tell you exactly how I knew that it wasn't right, but only that I was misunderstanding somehow. As this woman sat across from me, I simply said, "I am hearing Rachel, Rachel, Rachel, but I know that isn't quite right. Does that make any sense to you, a name like Rachel, but not Rachel?" She looked at me with a blank stare as tears began to well up in her eyes. "It's Rochelle, not Rachel. That is my daughter who died."

As soon as she acknowledged her daughter's name, the cool exterior, which I knew was merely a protective posture, immediately dissolved, and her tears flowed freely. With the tension gone, Rochelle was able to give me impressions of information for her mother who confirmed the information that I was able to communicate. I was relieved and grateful that I could open the door of her mother's heart and allow her daughter to express her love and gratitude for all that she had done for her, even as she took her last breath. She acknowledge that her mother was by her side as she slipped from this world, and confirmed that her mother has "seen something" quite extraordinary, and she wanted her mother to know that she had indeed seen her essence in the room as it gently released from her physical body.

Her mother described her as "radiant" as if her whole being had transformed before her eyes as she lay dying in her hospital bed. Then her mother saw a light come from her daughter's body and fill the room as she took her last breathe. Rochelle confirmed all of this for her Mom so that she could rest assured that she had indeed seen this blessed sight.

More and more as I worked with clients, both for energy healing and for Angel readings, I would receive information that would assist me in my work. At times, people would comment that they would begin to feel a "sense of peacefulness" as they entered my home. It was also beginning to become commonplace for clients to feel as if more than the two of us were in the room, with a sense that something very loving was with us.

Many times as people had energy healings they would ask, "How many pairs of hands do you have?" It became common for people to experience Angelic Beings gently hold their hand, or touch an area on their body where my hand had just been, as if to continue the healing in that area.

Whenever I work, I invite the Archangels and Honorable Ancestors to assist me, so that a healing can occur that will deeply affect the Body, Mind and Spirit of the person I am with. The Angels never let me down, and often, with their assistance, miraculous things would occur.

A YOUNG MAN'S WOUNDS IN AN OLD MAN'S BODY

*"So often we try to alter circumstances to suit ourselves,
instead of letting them alter us."*

Mother Maribel

I began getting invitations to speak with various groups about both Energy Medicine and Angels, ranging from medical groups to church organizations, and civic groups. When I speak with groups of people, it is my hope that they will be touched by what I had to say, and perhaps this information might change their perception about life, and what might be possible. It became common for individuals to open up and share experiences that they had not felt comfortable sharing with others. I hope to provide a safe place for others to share their wonderful experiences.

I was invited by a woman to come to her church to speak about the Angels. Gathering in the small church were fifteen to twenty people. I generally begin by asking those gathered if any of them had ever had an experience with an Angel before and usually two or three hands would go up. As I explained who the various Angels were and how they help us in our lives, the group sat quietly, occasionally someone would nod their head in agreement, some sat quietly with distance looks on their faces as if they were recalling memories. Many people had tears in their eyes. At the conclusion of the talk, the group was invited to enjoy coffee and desserts that the members had brought to share.

94

Often people would talk with me about some of their personal experiences, but it was one elderly gentleman, dressed in a lovely suit, who patiently waited for everyone else to walk away that touched my heart deeply.

Slowly the others got their food and sat talking in small groups. A quiet gentleman walked up to me and asked if we could talk. We moved to a more secluded location away from the others, and before he could speak, silent tears gathered in his eyes and quietly rolled down his cheeks. We sat quietly together holding hands as he gathered his composure. Finally he spoke.

"I have never told a single human being about this, but as you were standing in front of us speaking about the Angels, I knew that I had to share what I have carried in my heart for decades. As a young soldier I found myself in a war that I was not prepared for. My friends and I enlisted, feeling that it was the right thing to do. We thought it patriotic, wanting to defend our country. I could never have been prepared for what I would witness. I was sent to Europe during World War II. My platoon was overrun by German soldiers and to my horror my friends were being hit, one by one, by enemy fire.

We fought side by side, but for some reason I was not hit, but my friends lay dying on the cold ground around me. I felt frozen in time, not just from seeing my friends as they lay dead or dying, but from seeing Angels immediately by their sides as they lay praying on the ground, while other Angels stood by the dead men as if to help them know that everything would be okay. I have never told a single soul about what I saw on the battlefield. But I knew that I had to tell you today."

I was so moved by this moment. I asked why he had never spoken to anyone about seeing the Angels and he softly said, "I was sure that they would have thought that I was crazy, in fact, I was afraid that I might be." "Thank you so very much for honoring me with your experience. Yes, the Angels were very real and you did indeed see them. You were given a gift that day that few people ever witness. You were watching our Divine Helpers in action." There was nothing else to say. It was a gift to my heart.

As others became familiar with my work, time and again people would quietly ask if they could speak to me, and I was moved and awed by the many experiences that people have shared about their own Divine encounters. From the physician who could see Angels in the delivery room to a neurosurgeon who could see the synapses in the brain, like arcs of energy moving back and forth. Always, my question would be the same, "Do you tell others about this?" "No," was their common reply. Many people believe that they are the only ones having these remarkable experiences, and believe it or not, many more than you might expect have been touched by Divine Beings...our Angelic friends.

*Experience tries
to teach us that
the only important
thing is love.*

Sweet Andrea

"Mind cannot follow it,
nor words express her infinite sweetness."

Dante

My nephew Nicholas had found his soul mate, the love of his life, and now she lay dying in a hospital bed in Detroit, suffering from the debilitating side effects of chemotherapy and rejection of a stem cell transplant. Yet, through it all, she would say little of her suffering, and ask how others were doing.

Andrea and Nick had been together for fourteen years, and their love was extraordinary to watch. They helped one another in ways that most of us do not. Each had difficulty with some life skills, and rather that look at what one lacked, the other would simply take care of it so that the two of them could be as one unit, working together to be sure that the other felt whole.

You see, both Nick and Andrea are special needs adults. And each of them are blessed with extraordinary mothers. My dear sister Dianne, ever Nick's cheerleader, confidant and champion, struggled to make sure that her son would be able to function in the world, strengthening his skills and teaching him to believe in himself, even if things were hard. Andrea's mother, Rita, fought to have her precious daughter included in childhood activities that most take for granted. She opened Andrea's mind to many things, but most importantly, she clearly made sure that, even when excluded by others, she should never close her own heart. A drunk driver had killed Andrea's only brother and now Rita watched her only surviving child as she was losing her battle against leukemia.

While this was going on I struggled with whether on not I should travel to Sierra Madre, California to attend a weeklong workshop with Rosalyn L. Bruyere, gifted teacher and healer. Since Andrea had rallied in the past, I decided to go and to learn what I could from my mentor, and pray that no matter what happened, Andrea would be all right.

Each day while I was away I would call my sister to see how Andrea was doing. One evening, while sitting at the evening event, I clearly heard, "Andrea!" I looked to see what time it was and my watch said 9:00 pm. I quickly jotted the time down on my notebook and also wrote 12:00 am, indicating the three hours difference between our two locations. I silently said a prayer for her.

The next morning I received a phone call from Dianne. Tearfully, she told me that Andrea had died the night before. I asked her what time she had died and she said, "A little after midnight," with her beloved Nick, her mother and my sister by her side. I was stunned and immediately felt good bumps all over my body. Had Andrea spoken her own name to me the evening before? I knew that she had. Now I really began to have an internal struggle. Should I stay and continue with the workshop or return home to the funeral. Dianne told me to stay, that it would be okay. My heart was heavy, as I felt torn about what to do. Later, Andrea herself would share her thoughts with me.

That night, as I lay in bed thinking about Andrea, I was amazed to hear her voice. "Aunt Lainie, I'm good, I'm good, I'm good. You stay, this is important!" Tear flowed as our sweet girl gave her blessing for me to stay and learn what I could about healing the Body, Mind and Spirit so that I could come back and help others.

Through the waves of time and space Andrea was able to reach from one dimension to another, as always bringing love and comfort to another. Thanks, sweet girl.

THE MAN IN THE BATHROOM

"Do not weep, do not wax indignant.
Understand."

Baruch Spinoza
1632-1677

Sometimes the most remarkable things happen in the most un-usual places...when one is quietly sitting alone, driving a car, and even in a bathroom.

A woman had come to see me after having been referred by a friend. She had experienced the sudden death of her husband, and it had taken a toll on her. When she called I asked if she wanted to have an Angel Reading or an Energy Healing session. She was adamant that she did not want to have an Angel Reading; she was only interested in having Energy Healing done. To tell you the truth, I think that she was frightened by the notion that someone could hear from the other side, and she was having none of it. She was angry with him for dying, leaving her alone to raise their children, but, she did not want anyone to know those feelings.

Her debilitating grief was taking its toll on her health, and she wanted to get her energy back. I had just finished working with several clients in a row, so as she filled in her contact information form I excused myself to go to the bathroom. It's funny, but sometimes there is no escaping those that need to get their message across, regardless of what you might be doing. As I walked into the bathroom and closed the door, I distinctly heard a male voice say, "Mike."

Okay, I thought, who is Mike? A bit perplexed, I walked into the room where the woman was sitting and I asked, "Who is Mike?" She flashed an angry look at me and said, "Who told you his name?" I said, "Well, no one actually, unless you count the guy in the bathroom that just spoke to me." "Mike is my husband," she said. Holy smokes, he wasn't' taking "no" for an answer.

She had a bewildered look on her face as I began to explain that, although she was reluctant to receive any messages from the other side, her husband wanted to let her know that it was indeed him. In fact, I think that both of them were surprised that this stuff was actually real.

As he began to show me images of their three red-haired children, she could not deny what was happening, and she slowly allowed her anger to change to wonder. He brought messages about each one of them so that she would know that it was her husband, since I had never met her before and could not possibly know this information. He knew that she was angry with him for dying, and for her to have gone through the trauma of having to wake up and find her husband, who had been healthy the night before, dead in the bed beside her. How dare he do that to her, leaving the impact of that moment to scar her memory?

He profusely apologized for the way that it happened, and he assured her that it was not in his plans to leave at that time, but he wanted her to know that the experience was an amazing one. He felt no pain and had no fear as he fell asleep in one dimension and awoke in another. As her tears flowed you could see her anger disappear, as if her tears were washing away the sorrow and grief that had lined her face. Each tear seemed to soften her, and when she was done crying, she looked younger and more full of life.

All the while I continued doing an Energy Healing with her, which brought a higher frequency of energy into her body so that she could see things differently, and know that there was a healing going on in more ways than one. I was so grateful to witness this change.

LIGHTEN UP

*"God allows us to experience the low points of life
in order to teach us lessons
we could not learn in any other way."*

C. S. Lewis

By this time I had been doing face-to-face readings for over three years and I kept having a nagging feeling that I should be doing readings with groups of people. The debate would go back and forth in my mind…could I do it, should I do it, do I even want to do it?

I had attended audience readings and had watched them on television, but my nervousness about doing it held me back for a time. Often, I would hear the message before the presenter made their statement and it seemed as though this knowledge was pushing me along the road of Trust. As is usually the case, if you are meant to do something, God and the Angels will find a way to nudge you along, and this was no exception.

Various intuitive people that I know would often say to me, "Elaine, when are you going to do group readings?" Okay, okay, I get the message, I would think. Still, I would let other things fill my time. But before long, I finally understood why it might be of value for me to do group events.

There was a nagging feeling, my ego really, that would try to stop me in my tracks and not move forward with organizing an Audience Angel Reading. As you might suppose, the fears can be like a mountain to climb, but like any adventure we undertake in life we must first overcome our fears and when all is said and done we heave a huge sigh of relief and realize that it wasn't as bad as we had imagined! So I gathered my gumption and started to organize my first Audience Angel Reading. I was overwhelmed as the time drew nearer and I realized that sixty people would be there. What if I had nothing to say?

I should have known that it was not me, but rather Divine Beings who would be providing access to others in spirit as well as information about the individuals that I would work with. It was my job to be calm, trust, and then communicate the information. I needed to stop being a scardey cat about the whole thing. That was easy for them to say!

As a way to alleviate my concerns, the Angels instructed me to sit down to write their message, which I was to do before each audience reading. It was their way of setting the tone for the event. I realized that it was a pretty darn good idea, so as I had promised, I sat at my computer the day of the reading and asked to receive their message. I am always amazed at the eloquence of their messages, and I now look forward to each and every one of them. The following is the message from my first Audience Angel Reading.

Message received on March 23, 2006:
I was told that this loving message was from Archangel Gabriel, the Angel of Communication.

"Say these words this evening to those who come to hear. It is their own precious hearts that are in need of truth, understanding and most of all, Love. It is the human condition at this time that has made Our Presence known to so many. It is true that we have

always been among you, even in your darkest hours. It was then, and it is now, that you have the opportunity to see yourselves anew. To begin to appreciate you as we appreciate you. You all have come to this Earth to bring a message. We are not the only messengers of God. Each and every one of you are as well.

Bring the love that is your birthright back to your own precious heart. It has been for far too long that you have pushed Love aside. Your condition of love is not the real Essence of Love. The condition of love that we speak of tonight is the condition that brings about mistrust and pain. That is your misperception of love. It is the deepest longing within your sweet soul to know the Love that brings forth joy, your natural state of being. It is not natural for you to be so heavy of heart; it is, unfortunately though, your impression of normal.

What is whole and vibrant and brings joy to the world is natural and best. How can this be changed, you ask? Starting within each and every one of you. Let tonight be a beginning. This is not about asking you to change all circumstances of your life, for this is not possible or helpful. But you can, in any given moment of time, change how you respond to one another and to your own self. Look with kind and loving eyes upon your own being. It has done great things for you.

It has brought you to this moment in time in which you can breathe and feel and know that these struggles that you hold so dear to you are of little value to your greater understanding. You can only learn the lessons of life when you walk through and away from the pain that you have held so dear. It does not serve you to take years to learn the lessons of love. Learn these lessons every day, and bring the Essence of Life, the Essence of Love forth.

Put aside all that you think that you know for this evening. Allow yourself to be open to new possibilities, to new horizons, to new joys and understandings. Be willing, once and for all, to know how precious you are. There is not one being here who is not precious in the eyes of God. It is you who lack that vision.

It is with great joy that we accompany you on this journey called Life. Call upon us at all times. Know that this is not an abdication of your responsibility or will, but rather the call to a trusted and loving friend, who will be honest and gentle, who will help you to see with new eyes and hear with new ears so that the greater meaning of things can be understood.

When understanding is attained then wisdom can be employed. The Essence of your Being, Dear Ones is one thing and one thing only, and that is Love. Begin to know Love in its truest form and your life will unfold for you in ways you have only dreamed of."

I knew, without a doubt, that the message that they provided that evening helped to alleviate my own fears of trying to bring messages to 60 people in two hours. I needn't have worried, since my sole purpose was to listen and then communicate everything that I was seeing, hearing, feeling and knowing. They allowed the information to flow freely, and in that evening, every single person received a message. By the end of the evening, I was exhilarated and exhausted, more from nerves than from doing any strenuous work. As time progressed and I became more comfortable with the process of doing group readings, I felt much more trusting and at peace, and in turn the information would begin to flow without much effort from me.

I am always amazed during the course of the evening's events that the message that the Angels have provided are acutely poignant for the evening's gathering. That particular night there was a young woman in the audience to whom I was immediately drawn. She had a forlorn look on her face, and although I do not always recall all of the messages that are given to everyone, there are certain ones that stand out in my mind.

I recall being drawn to her, and looking at her with a sense of compassion, I said, "Why are you so angry? It is time for you to be willing to bring joy back into your life." The words were spoken with care and some lightheartedness. She looked stunned and a bit upset. Then clearly I was told to reiterate the information, suggesting to her that she be more joyful, that she had a choice to be angry and a choice to be happy and that anger would eventually get the best of her. She abruptly got up and walked out of the room. I felt badly since I know that the Angels were asking her to "Lighten Up," both literally and figuratively, for her own benefit. I silently prayed that the message would slowly enter her heart so that joy could find a home.

As I walked up to various people I would pause for a moment and then begin to hear information. There was a gentleman in the front row and as I stood next to him, there was an elderly gentleman in spirit wishing to convey a message to him. I kept hearing an "O" name, like "Oscar," although I knew that was not exactly right. Rather than go through a list of male names that begin with "O," I simply asked, "Do you know a man whose name begins with the letter "O," like Oscar or something? It feels as though he is on your father's side. It sounds like a foreign name. Do you know who this might be?" I asked. He looked a bit stunned and quietly said, "His name is Omar, and yes, I know who you are talking about. It is my father." I love it when I am able to get close to the name right off the bat. Omar lovingly gave messages to his son, and as he did I could see a change in the man in front of me, as if a greater awareness and understanding of his father had just washed away years of confusion. It was beautiful to witness.

I recall walking up to a woman and asked her if she was a nurse. "I just was accepted at nursing school," she said. The Angels wanted her to know that school would not be as hard as she thought, and that she would be an angel to many people in her nursing career. They thanked her for listening to her own heart and stepping into this important role with confidence.

The Angels would help me by providing words of encouragement to help a young woman believe in herself and from a deceased father to let his son know that he loved him and was proud of the man that he had become. Even though in life the father was not able to communicate that important message, he was saying it now. It is never too late.

Guide gently
with your
hand and heart.
Remember that the spirit is a
fragile thing.

REMEMBERING WHY

*"To be surprised, to wonder,
is to begin to understand."*

Jose Ortega y Gasset

The next Audience Angel Reading was on May 11, 2006 and their message for that evening was short and profound, yet another reminder that the Angels are with us at all times. This is the message from that evening.

May 11, 2006, Written at 12:49 pm:

"Most holy and beloved friends, your presence here tonight is one that brings great joy to the kingdom that is both on earth as is it in heaven. The joy that is felt is our rejoicing at your soul's willingness to learn and grow. We are your Divine friends and assistants in this life's journey."

This evening's reading was unique for me. Some of my own precious sisters were in attendance and I was a bit nervous, hoping that they would see that I wasn't making all of this stuff up, and that I could somehow be of benefit to them. When I know someone well, I am generally not too keen on doing a reading for them, since I am concerned that I might be influenced by what I already know, and might be unable to give an accurate reading. I should not have been concerned.

As was the pattern from the last reading, once I read the Angel's message the nervous feeling would completely vanish and I would be drawn to one person or another and then the information would begin to flow. Once a message was conveyed, the Angels would gently direct my attention to another person. I would stand next to the individual and within moments begin to get information for them.

As I went from person to person, in no particular order, I finally came to my sister Therese. I know and love my sister, who in truth is my stepsister, but over the course of the thirty-two years that our parents were married to one another she became not only my stepsister but my true sister of the heart, a trusted friend and I love her dearly. I knew that she had not been feeling well and that the last few years had been very difficult for our family, as we had experienced three deaths. First was my father on December 19, 2003, then Therese's mother, one year and one day later, on December 20, 2004 and then on March 19, 2005, my stepbrother John, Therese's brother, had died as a result of many years of self-abuse. As a nurse, she was often the one who was called to give assistance to him. It had taken its toll on her.

John was a good man, but a very troubled man, and his self-abusive behavior caused the decline of many areas of his life. He was truly brilliant intellectually, and had a keen love for anything to do with Native American culture. He knew more than most historians about their lives and their civilizations. So it was not surprising to me that John came with a message for Therese. She had stood by his side, even in some of his darkest hours, when others would not.

Since we know each other so well, any message that he might give that night would have to be something that I would have no knowledge of. And as it turned out, that is exactly what happened.

As John knew that his life was coming to an end, he began to give special things away to those he knew would appreciate them. And that night, when I went over to Therese, John made his presence very clear to me. He told me to tell her that he had given her a special gift, and then proceeded to describe it in great detail. She acknowledged that he had privately given something to her as a gift and she knew exactly what it was that he was referring to. He wanted her to know that she was using it improperly, and that it was intended to be a totem, something that she should not share with others. She began to cry and said that she had indeed been sharing this gift with others, and did not realize that a totem was a personal item. She wept and then smiled.

After giving Therese her message, I was drawn to a woman sitting two seats from her. Funny thing, but when the Angels want me to know that someone has a question that they would like to ask, they literally show me a question mark above their head. As I approached her I asked if she had a question. She looked at me and asked, "My husband and I are trying to get pregnant. Can you tell me if I am going to have a baby?"

Within a second the Angels told me to say the following. *"We want you to remember why you love your husband. Conceiving a child should never be a chore, but rather should be an act of love. Let the fear of not conceiving go and remember why you love one another. Bring fun back into your relationship. Go on a date, and let yourselves feel the love that you have for one another. Remember why you want to have a child with this man, your husband."* The words were said with a great deal of care, trying to be conscious of conveying their message accurately and with compassion.

It's All About Love

"There was nothing remote or mysterious here -
only something private.
The only secret was the ancient communication
between two people."

Eudora Welty

The following morning I was a bit stunned when I received an angry email from the woman I had spoken to the previous evening about conceiving a child. She thought that I had been very harsh and that the way that I had presented the information was very unkind. All I could think was, "Geez, were we at the same event last night?" I felt very badly and apologized if I had offended her in any way, but I had to tell her that it was my responsibility to convey the message as accurately as I could. I was perplexed and concerned, since it is not in my nature to intentionally hurt another.

About a month later I was invited to a house warming party for a young woman that I knew who had just moved into her new home. I knew that I would not be able to stay very long so I made it a point to arrive early to the party so that I could stay for a reasonable amount of time. As the time approached for me to leave and I was saying my goodbyes to the hostess and others at the gathering, the woman from the reading happened to be coming into the house. She stopped in her tracks. We both gingerly approached one another and before I could speak, she said, "Elaine, can I speak with you privately?" "Of course, let's go outside," I said.

As we stood together on the front porch she said to me, "I owe you an apology for the unkind email that I sent to you. I was so angry with you, because my husband and I had been trying to get pregnant and it was becoming frustrating. I took what you said as an insult. Well, a few days later, I realized that perhaps you were right, and that we were making getting pregnant a job rather than a pleasure. We decided to go out on a date, to truly remember what we loved about each other. And, I want to tell you that you were right, and, I am going to have a baby. I want to thank you for being willing to say what you did, it was what I needed to hear." I was so happy to hear that, and we both hugged one another. This was wonderful news. As I got in my car and drove away, I thanked the Angels out loud… "You guys are so cool!"

I realized a very valuable lesson that evening, and that is that if I am to have any sense of integrity in this work then I cannot filter or edit what I am being told. I have to trust the validity and the purpose of the message. I am glad that I learned that lesson and I am glad to say that she and her husband now have two beautiful, healthy children and their lives are full of love and compassion for one another, as it should be.

A MESSAGE TO HER MOTHER

*"I was gratified to be able to answer promptly.
I said I don't know."*

Mark Twain

June 19, 2006 was the evening of my fourth Audience Reading. Again the Angels had everything in perfect Divine order.

That evening, instead of walking around the room with a microphone in my hand, I asked those in attendance if they would mind if we were more informal and they all readily agreed. This was an especially unique group, and I was trying not to panic too much, since this group was very small, only six in attendance. Four of the six people were new to me, and as they sat in a semi-circle in front of me, I read the Angel's message for the evening, and as always, I was to understand later just how perfect that message was for those in attendance that evening.

June 19, 2006 message for Audience Angel Reading

"Dearest Friends, Life has its ups and downs. Some bring joy while others bring worry and concern. Still others bring puzzlement and fear. It is time to learn to ride the ups and downs of life as an observer.

Throughout your precious life, we have watched you and stood by your side...every moment has been observed, shared and blessed. If for one moment you could remember to see with your

Divine eyes, you would let troubles pass you by, like a passenger on a ship observing the land as you pass the shore. Every event is truly an observable moment, one which is not meant to label your outlook, but rather to help you glean information about the whole.

When you observe what appears to be an "up" moment, many of you may hold onto it with a fearful heart that you will soon be experiencing loss. You do not trust the moment, and therefore the joy of the moment may be lost too soon. And because of that response you learn not to trust the "up" moments and make the error of only trusting its opposite. Yet, when you experience what appears to be a "down" moment, you grab it and hold it close to you, as if it is happening to you, rather than being an observer. This "down" moment has become the defining moment for many. Many describe their lives by the "downs" that have occurred. Would it not be wiser to hold this moment at arm's length, so that it can be viewed for what it is? It is merely a moment in time, not a definition of a soul.

So, dear friends, change your point of view. An "up" or a "down" is not the navigator of your life. That, my dear, is your sole purpose, to be the navigator of your Life. Ride the wave to get to your destination. Trust that life is full of many still moments that neither define nor shape you. This precious life is lived fully when you ride the wave of time, as a peaceful observer, sending love where love is not, and being a bringer of love to every situation. It is not as hard as it seems. If you think back, and remember from where you came, you will be able to see yourself as we see you. You will know that Love is truly all there is. Have that precious moment be your defining moment. When unconditional love is remembered, even for a moment, the gift it holds can bring peace, love and joy to all of your days."

After reading the message, I "listened" for a moment and my attention was drawn to the woman sitting directly in front of me. I asked her name and she quietly said, "Mary." Immediately there was an impression of a young woman standing to her left side, and I asked, "Mary, please excuse me if I am wrong, but do you have a daughter that passed away, and she is making me feel like it was some time ago. Does this make sense to you?" With a shocked looked on her face, Mary quietly said, "Yes, this is my daughter."

Her daughter wanted me to let her mother know that she did not die of what they had thought she had died of. "Mary, does it make sense that your daughter would say that she did not die of what you had thought? She is rubbing her thumb and index finger together as if to indicate a tiny problem. She is saying that she had a tiny defect in her heart and that there was nothing that anyone could have done about it. She wants you to know that this is what caused her death. Does this make any sense to you?" I asked.

Mary looked so startled as she said, "I was told that there was no known cause of death. She had gone to bed as usual, and in the morning had not gotten up to go to school. When I went to her room to wake her, I found her dead in her bed." My heart broke for her. As soon as this information was exchanged, the floodgates of information came quickly, giving Mary additional information about her family.

Just like other readings, every person received messages that night, and it seemed that I had not failed after all. Just the right people were there that evening, and I was able to spend more time with each person in the two hours allotted for the group reading.

expect a miracle

HEALING A WOUNDED HEART

"When such as I cast out remorse
So great a sweetness flows into the breast
We must laugh and we must sing,
we are blest by everything,
Everything we look upon is blest."

W. B. Yeats

I received a call from Mary, asking if I would consider doing a group reading in her home. I had not done that before, but there wasn't any reason why I couldn't, so I accepted the invitation. Mary's home was full of love. You could feel it squeezing itself into every corner of her home. As I arrived, Mary and the many people who gathered in her townhouse lovingly greeted me.

"Before you came Elaine, we were talking and we wondered if you would consider changing the format somewhat. If you don't mind, we would each like to have a private reading, so perhaps you could tell us all about what it is that you do and then you could give twenty minute private readings. Would that be okay with you?" Mary asked. I tried to quickly calculate the number of people and how long it would take to do private readings. I agreed, and Mary promised that she would have a wonderful Irish meal for me afterwards. How could I refuse?

As I sat in her living room I couldn't help but notice the woman sitting directly across from me. Her body language was very closed, with her arms crossed tightly against her chest, her legs crossed and with a look on her face that conveyed her thoughts,

"What I am doing here? This is nonsense." All of a sudden while I looked at her I heard a phrase in my mind, "This woman is a nun." Oh boy, here we go…

After I told the group how the whole experience began for me, Mary indicated that it would be quieter and much more private if I went to the lower level of her home to do the private readings. She showed me the way and I prepared the tape recorder for the first session. I don't recall the exact order, but before long it was time for the "nun" to come downstairs for her reading.

As she sat across from me, I heard once again, "This woman is a nun." So, I asked, "Are you a nun? Your energy feels very much like a nun." "No," she said, "I am not a nun, but I have taught religious education for over thirty years." Good enough for me, I thought.

Now, I would like to explain how some things "come" to me. Sometimes a thought just pops into my head, other times I might hear a name or phrase repeating in my mind, other times I "see" something in my mind's eye. And that is what happened next.

All of a sudden I "saw" my deceased stepmother Jane in my mind's eye. By way of example, imagine that as you are looking at this page, you can also envision someone's face. You know that you are looking at the pages of a book, but you can clearly "see" someone in your mind's eye. That is what it is like to "see." So as I was sitting across from her, all of a sudden my stepmother Jane appeared in my field of vision, slightly to my right.

I thought, "Jane, what the heck are you doing here?" Now, I know that people often want to help from the other side, but I was a bit perplexed. But Jane would not go away. Perhaps there is something that I need to say here. So I looked at the woman seated in front of me and I said, "This might sound odd, but then again, all of this might sound odd. However, I have to tell you that my deceased stepmother keeps showing herself to me. I am getting the feeling that she wants me to say something to you. Do you happen to know a woman by the name of Jane Wolford Hughes?"

The "nun's" face began to immediately soften, and she had a surprised smile on her face. "Jane Wolford Hughes? I loved Jane Wolford Hughes! I used to work for her. She was the best boss that I ever had!" Holy garbanzo beans! (One of Jane's favorite expressions.) "Well," I said, "Jane is my stepmother. My dad and her were married for over thirty years." With that confirmation of her knowing Jane, her entire demeanor changed. She was no longer closed to me and information began to flow effortlessly. I later learned that not only had she known my stepmother, but also our hostess, Mary, knew and respected Jane. Thanks dolly!

Those twenty minutes flew swiftly by. She thanked me and gave me a hug before leaving the room to get the next person. I could hear her excited tones as she talked to the others upstairs. The next reading would be an experience that I will never forget.

Within a few minutes a quiet woman by the name of Ellan came downstairs. She looked a bit timid, not sure of what to expect. Immediately I felt the presence of a female and she was indicating that she was on the maternal side. "There is a woman here, on your mother's side. She is repeating a "M" name, do you know a Mary, Martha, Margaret, some "M" name?" She looked blankly at me and said, "No." "Are you sure, she is saying that you know her, and that she has an M name. She is on your mother's side."

"Could it be my mother?" she asked. Well, as soon as she asked that question I had the most intense pain in my mouth, starting on the left side, going through my tongue to the right side, with a searing pain in my right jaw and then in my right ear. It took my breath away. "Oh my goodness, I am having a very intense pain, that just came on. Does this make any sense to you as it relates to your mother?"

She looked stunned, and I know that I was. "Yes, it makes sense to me," was her reply. As soon as she acknowledged this I heard very clearly, "I killed myself with a gun in my mouth." Oh, my God, how can I say that, what if I am wrong? But I knew that I had to say it.

"Please forgive me if I am wrong, but did your mother kill herself with a gun in her mouth?" She looked at me and quietly said, "Yes, she did." Then I heard, "Please tell my daughter that I did not die immediately, it took five seconds for me to die, long enough for me to know that I had made a terrible mistake. Please ask her to forgive me." We both sat there stunned. Never had I had a message of this intensity to give to someone, and never had I felt the impact of the person's actions. I began to understand that it was the only way that her daughter would know, without a single doubt, that it was her mother there with us that evening.

The information continued to come. My client explained to me that she was only ten years old when this tragedy occurred and at the time of the reading she was fifty-six. Ellan had realized that there might have been many unknown problems that led to her mother's suicide. It was my hope that this information brought her peace.

Her mother asked that she talk to her siblings and ask them to forgive her. There was such intense remorse for her actions and a longing to let her children know that she loved them and that she wanted each of them to know how much. Those twenty minutes were very intense, with a mixture of pain, sorrow, joy and love. I was so grateful to be able to share the message from a mother to her daughter. Having lost my own mother when I was thirteen, I could truly feel the pain of her mother's death. It took several hours for the pain to completely subside, and each time I relayed the experience to others the pain would come back for a time.

After completing the last reading for the evening, I sat at the dining table with Mary, her family and friends. I could feel the incredible love that they had for one another, and I felt a special blessing that day. They had embraced me with the kind of love that only a family member could feel. They made me feel like one of their own. As we sat around Mary's table I learned that she too had known my stepmother Jane. My, oh my, it is amazing how things come together!

So, that Audience Angel Reading, in which I thought that I had failed in some way because there were only six people in attendance, confirmed for me that there are no mistakes, and that the exact number of people who were meant to be there, were there. My job was to trust, convey the messages, and allow the healing to begin.

Within a few days of the reading at Mary's house, Ellan contacted me. She asked me if I would be willing to come to Charlotte, North Carolina, to do readings for her friends. I did not know until her call that she and her husband, Mary's eldest son, had flown in from Charlotte to be at the reading at Mary's house that night. And, that one of the other people in attendance that night was also from out of town. I am glad that I did not know, since I would have been very concerned about whether their trip had been worthwhile. Within a matter of weeks, I was in Ellan and GB's home, and I am grateful to say that it felt like family to me.

Imagine...

MOVING THROUGH SPACE AND TIME

*"Enjoy what you can,
and endure what you must."*

Johann Wolfgang von Goethe

Sometimes it is hard to imagine how things are so intertwined, but they certainly are. Our concept of time and space is so very limited. We think of time in a linear fashion; there is the past, the present and the future. Yet, as I do this work I have been able to understand that time is so much more than a line moving in one direction. It is more than mere snapshots of events, memories and experiences. It is the whole kit and caboodle, all at once. Can you imagine that?

Imagine, in the snap of a finger, centuries blend into one moment, and everything is there for our understanding, all in one down-loadable moment. That is why I am constantly amazed, awed and thrilled to get a glimpse of the magnificence of God's creative process, of which we are an integral part, if we only choose to get into the game. By game I don't mean in any way to slight the creative Genius that we can witness, if we put our guard down. Then once again, we might be able to see that it all comes together in a snap…just like magic.

The Angels often use the day's events to illustrate what would be shared in an Audience Angel Reading. They remind me that the dimensions of time pose no limitations and that evening I would understand that time and space could indeed be traversed in the

126

blink of an eye. That evening, with the assistance of the Angels, I would witness one woman thank her family for their loving support and hear a gentleman give a "pat on the back" to his old buddy. Friendship and love know no bounds of time.

I heard this from the Angels:

"Being here, being there. In the concept of time and space, you might begin to understand our connection to you, to the Divine Center of your being and to your creative self.

Even today, as you moved through time and space from one part of the country to another, using your very common mode of transportation (an airplane), consider that just 100 short years ago this concept would have been considered absurd.

Time and Space are not defined with the same meaning that you hold now that was held then. Seemingly, the same is true for you, here and now…and what may be a totally unknown reality weeks or months from now may be soon considered common, yet beyond your grasp at the moment.

As you wake in one state and sleep in another this is analogous to dimensions of time. Those beings that have lived and are now not living in your current perception, have merely moved from one state to another…Awakening in the human experience and falling asleep in another.

We simply move through time and space with more efficiency than you currently do. That will change as your perception changes. Reach back in a moment's memory and see everything new again. Just as you clear your vision when you wake to a new day, clear your vision once again as you wake to a new perception. Open your heart, and truths will be revealed."

My friend Sally was in the audience that evening, along with her mother and her sister. After reading the message from the Angels that night, I could feel that there was someone who had been at a funeral that day. So, I asked, "Has anyone been to a funeral lately?" One look at Sal's face and I could see that the message was for her. "Oh, my gosh, Elaine, all three of us were at my aunt's funeral... today!"

The expression on her face was priceless. As it turned out it was her mother's sister-in-law who had been buried that very day. She wanted her family to know how happy she was, how peaceful her passing had been and that it was nothing like she had expected. She was so grateful for all of the kind words that had been said about her, and most importantly, she didn't want anyone to be sad. She was fine, and she loved them all very much.

As I made my way around the room, I was drawn to a gentleman sitting on my far left. I had never met the man before or the woman sitting by his side. Generally what occurs as I am directed to an individual is that I pause for a moment, often closing my eyes, and within a few seconds I begin to get messages. As I approached the gentleman I felt the strong presence of a soldier, a young man who had died during the Vietnam War. The soldier showed himself to me in his khaki uniform, looking handsome, young and healthy. He said that he had a short name and that he wanted to give a message to his friend.

I looked at the gentleman as he sat quietly, and I began to speak. "There is a young man here, who appears to be a soldier from the Vietnam War. He is saying that you were friends and that he wants you to know that he is fine. He is saying that you have been thinking a great deal about him and he says that he has a three letter name. Does this make any sense to you?" Looking a bit stunned, but happy at the same time, he said, "Yes, it is my friend Ron. I have been thinking of him all day long, hoping that he would be able to communicate with me this evening. This is incredible!"

Tears welled up in his eyes as the woman next to him quietly took his hand. "He was my best friend in high school and we were very close. I felt so terrible that he had died and a bit guilty that I had not had the chance to say goodbye."

Ron wanted to reassure his friend that all was fine. That he did not suffer at the moment of his death and that he was often near his friend. Ron asked that his friend take better care of himself and to treasure every moment that he had on Earth. It is the greatest gift we could ever have.

THE ANGELS AND ME

The Season of Goodness

*"Imagine for yourself a character,
a model personality,
whose example you determine to follow,
in private as well as in public."*

Epictetus

I had been invited to speak to a group of women in Windsor, Ontario. It was a cold December night in 2006, but the warmth of the group gathered there quickly warmed my heart. With approximately forty people in attendance, I began by reading the Angel's message.

"Deep within the Hearts of Mankind, there resides a reservoir of Love and Compassion that is beyond your comprehension. Yet, there is never a moment in time in which this reservoir is beyond your reach.

Through the eons of time, humans have fought for their belief in being right, in being in charge and we can promise you that this is humanity's worst battle. The battle that rages within each and every one of you is an illusion. The illusion of separation, of lack, of not enough Love to go around, of not enough Time…the illusion has many facets, each one as false as the next.

You are in the midst of a Holy Season, not one confined to any religion or any particular sect of people. But rather, a Holy Sea-

son, in which mankind opens it hearts to each other. This is the most natural state for any Spirit to experience; in fact it is the only true state of Being.

Foolishly, particular times have been set-aside in your calendar of days, in the segments of time that you call a Season. It is during these times that you open your hearts and homes, you give gifts and receive gifts, but often you fail to see that each and every moment is a Season in Time, a precious opportunity to experience Love, both the giving and the receiving. Open your lives to the Season of Goodness.

This Season, dear Ones, is too limited for the reality of Love. There is no Season of Love - there is Only Love. The precious time that you set aside for family and friends to be remembered was never meant to occur only on Special Occasions. Your entire Existence, Your Every Breath, Each Beat of Your Holy Heart is a Special Occasion. Know this, and your life will begin to take on new meaning, new urgency to express kindness, love, humility, generosity, reverence, awe and wonder - all of which are aspects of Love.

In this Season, open your hearts and your homes as you have done in years past, but as the adornments are tucked away, never put your Love away with the decorations. Let every moment bring Light, let every heart that knows your own sing in unison with you. In moments of quite thought, be an ornament of Love. Let Light shine out of your blessed eyes to light the way for yourself and others, so that you will know the warmth of Love's Eternal Flame.

Let each gift that you give be surrounded with your gift of Love, and let every gift that you receive remind your heart that each moment is a gift, each breath is a wonder, and every tear of joy

*and love and tenderness is a perfect diamond of human expres-
sion. Your Life is Your Season of Love and Light. So at the end
of your human days, you will see the moments of your human existence and you will see yourself shine like the magnificent Light
of Love that you are."*

There were women of great insights in the group, some of whom
used their gifts and others who did not. I was drawn to one
woman and, pausing for a moment asked, "Are you an artist?"
She shook her head "No," while her two friends beside her shook
their heads "Yes." "Well, are you an artist?" I asked. She was
reluctant to acknowledge her talents, but the Angels wanted her
to know that this gift should not be kept inside, but used to create
beauty for the world to see. You never know until you try. And
I can speak from experience here. As an artist myself, I recall
the feelings of pure joy at creating something out of only my
imagination, paper, colors, pens and brushes.

Finally, the woman acknowledged that, although she would not
call herself an artist, she did enjoy painting. "Good, now the Angels want you to know that it is time to create and display your
works publicly...you can do it!"

There were other women in the group that the Angels wanted me
to encourage to believe in themselves so that others would be able
to benefit from and be inspired by their actions. Then I noticed
a beautiful red-haired woman in the group. As I approached her,
the Angels wanted me to thank her for all the people that she had
helped with her intuitive gifts, and to let her know that she was
far from done with the work she was to do. They were grateful
for her being willing to "show up and serve."

A few months later I received an email from one of the women
that I had spoken to at the event in Windsor. I love it went some-

one takes the time to let me know how the information given had affected their life. The following is her email to me.

"I was at your Angel Reading at Iona College in Windsor in December 2006. It was a wonderful evening - as you walked through the room you approached me and said I was an artist -- I said no I wasn't, and two friends sitting near me objected and said yes I was--- I thought that was funny, and I agree that I work in writing and marketing, also dance, and sing with community theatre -- but never considered myself an artist -- I always associate that with people who draw, paint, sculpt, etc.

In February I started an art class at a community centre called "Colour Play" using one colour each week that relates to the Chakras . After two classes the teacher asked us to select pieces to enter into a juried show at the Windsor Art Gallery -- I was going on a trip the next day -- so I hurried and selected two pieces, went to Wal-Mart for frames and wrote an artist statement to accompany the work and left them for the teacher to submit.

Two weeks later arriving home from Mexico on Friday at midnight, I had a phone message from the Art Gallery to say both pieces had been selected. My $100.00 ticket to the black tie event would be at the door -- and an invitation to attend the reception for sponsors and artists. I did indeed attend (by myself) - I couldn't get a ticket for my husband at that late date. It was an extraordinary evening. Everyone looked very elegant in black and white, and I was certainly glad that I chose a simple black evening dress, I didn't realize the event was titled "Everything Isn't Always Black and White."

The curator discussed 6 pieces of the 35 displayed and two of them were mine! I later learned that of the couple of hundred artists who submitted, I was the only one who had both pieces se-

135

lected. This was all a very heady experience.

This was all very new to me, I was also paid as an exhibitor by the Gallery - so I guess now I can say, "I am an artist." And you were right when you addressed me as such, many months before it came to be."

I believe that the Angels were asking us all to pay attention to the "gifts" that we bring into this life and the ones that seemingly "blossom" in their own time. Using the gifts of insight and creativity are just some of the ways that we can bring our gifts into the Light, and allow those gifts to be shared with others on this journey called Life.

BE THE GIFT

"Light tomorrow with today."

Elizabeth Barrett Browning

Audience Reading Message December 11, 2006 - 7:58 am:

"Look, really look, around you. Look at the beauty and the wonder and the big and the small. Look and see the wonders that surround you each and every moment of your life. In this busy time, in this Season of Change, resist the temptation to rush through your day. Getting everything done is not as important and filling yourself with Love.

Examine your thoughts about this precious time of year. Many look to the birth of the Great Being of Light known as Jesus the Christ. Many fill their days with the desire for gift giving. Many hope that the gifts that they desire will be the gifts that they will receive.

We ask you, this evening, to change your focus, beginning this night, and become aware of the Gifts of Light and Love that are your dearest treasures. They are your birth-gifts, they are your treasured wonders to explore and know about your own Divine Beginnings. This treasured gift is within your Heart. Examine it, share it, embrace it, and live the Light of it fully.

You, like our precious Brother who's Life is celebrated in this Season of Light, are also a Being of Light. You are made of the same

137

things. You come from the Great Center of the Heart of the Most High. We do not speak in your terms of religious context here, for that is where the story has taken many roads, yet the roots of the True Understanding are taken from the same Source.

In this Season, expand your awareness of the purpose of your Precious Life. Know that this season is not only for the celebration of One Birth, but for Your Birth as well. Let your Heart birth wonder, kindness, humility, warmth, trust, patience, tenderness, and solitude. Let the Great Star in the Sky illuminate your Life, as it foretold of the birthplace of Our Brother, let it also foretell of the wonder you will bring to the Earth beginning this day.

Know, as Our Brother knew, that your life in this present incarnation is limited in the number of days you will walk this Sacred Earth. In this life, express goodness; cause others to look within themselves as they observe your existence. Shine your Light, not as a spotlight for others to see you, but rather as a lamppost to guide the way. Cause others to see the Goodness that is born in the Hearts of Humankind.

As you gift each other with beautiful and wonderful things, let your most prized gift be the Gift of your Loving Presence. With every step, bring Love forth. With every Breath, let peace be present. With every song you hear, bring the melody of forgiveness forward to let that be the blessed gift you bring. Be The Gift, this day and every day hence. You too are a Light for the World. Let this Holy Land in which you live glow with the warmth of your Human Heart so that as you are viewed from on High, may you shine like a most magnificent gift, reflecting back to the Creator the gifts of your precious Birth."

That message says it all.

Let a kind word be said

THE POWER OF A LOVING HEART

"Forget injuries, never forget kindnesses."

Confucius

February 20, 2007, Angel Message - 4:22 pm:

"Within you lies the power to do great and glorious things. You are as much a part of God's divine plan as we are. The separation you perceive is an illusion, a non-truth, and a disempowering illusion that has brought you to your knees, both literally and figuratively, when in truth you should be shouting from the rooftops.

Do not allow yourselves to be deemed "unworthy" any longer. In this lifetime it is your great opportunity to see greatness and know that it is not a power to be used but rather a gift to be embraced. When you know who you are you will never stoop to allow others to forget who they are too. You are Divine expressions of the Love of God. You are powerful beyond your knowing, and your use of this power, in loving and peaceful ways, will bring the Loving Energy of God to be always at your disposal. There is no time when you cannot be your greatest self; it is only through your belief in such falsehood that you have disempowered yourself and those around you. This must end in order for you to step into your glorious self.

Using this power allows for Grace - the power of God in action in your human life, to be your calling card. Have it precede you in your actions, words and deeds, and let it be the parting gift that you leave behind with every individual and situation.

It is only when others begin to see, through your example, what the Power of Love truly means, that they can lay down the armaments of their own woundings and walk in the Glorious Light of Love and Peace.

You have all been disempowered, at various times in your lives, by disease, illness, injury and grief. This energy imbalance does not need to stay with you, but rather used as a time of self-examination, not bitterness and worry. Know that you are always connected to an endless River of Energy, which can lift you, body and soul, to your next great understanding of your own existence. You are not powerless unless you choose to be so. Make another choice if this has been your habit. Teach yourself today to see your true worth.

Does a beautiful bird fly through the sky and rest on the branch of a tree and say to itself, "I am not worthy to be here."? Of course it does not. Nor should you, dear friends. Your life is valuable beyond measure, whether you choose to see it while you are living or wait until after you have breathed your last. Do not waste your precious moments, each a gift to your soul of awareness and love.

As you bring your awareness to the Power of Love, your gift to this life is to not allow unloving ways to be in your presence. Do not stand by when anyone is unkind and let it pass, giving it permission to be there and to continue. Any act of unkindness that is not called to an act of Love has been given permission to be in your presence, thus disempowering you and all around you. Stop unkindness in its tracks.

Shine Love where unkindness has been allowed to spread. Take a Stand of Love so that you become a presence where nothing but Love is welcomed. Be vigilant. Be strong. Be powerful in your Presence of Love. Accept nothing else, and soon you will find that you have changed your world.

When you know that your Existence is not by Accident, when you know that Love is where you are because you choose it to be so, you will have stepped into your Power. The Power that Brings the Greatest Force to bear...The Power of a Loving Heart will change this World and all of the dimensions in which you reside."

It is humbling when you begin to understand that circumstances that you have not even dreamed of are in the works, weaving together events that ultimately bring people together. Sometimes we need many nudges before we make a move in the direction of caring for ourselves, but when we do take that step, remarkable things begin to occur.

A beautiful woman came to see me, and truly, beautiful is not an adequate adjective. Stunning would be more like it. We often make the error of judging a book by its cover, and we do that all of the time with people. A beautiful person must have had a charmed life, since they appear to be so comfortable and capable. But sometimes, beneath the surface, there is a wounded soul whose exterior hides the trauma that one has experienced, and which deeply affects the way they view themselves and their place in the world. Yet when one can see through and beyond their troubled past and look with joy and enthusiasm to the gifts that they can bring into their own lives, then truly a miracle has occurred.

The Angel's message above speaks to just this type of change that must take place in the human heart before we are able to see ourselves differently, and not just through the eyes of the trauma that we have known. The following is a clear example of how the Angels can and will be persistent in making sure that we open our eyes and our hearts and treasure the gifts that this life can bring, so that we can be all that we are meant to be.

The following is an experience from a client that I'll call N.L.

"...They say, "When the student is ready, the teacher appears..." I find this is true for healing. If a person is not open or accessible to the idea of healing, it cannot take place. No one can determine this timing but the Self and the Spirit. Elaine came into my life by flyer, handed to me from a nurse taking her class. The fact that continuing education credits (CEU hours) in the nursing field were provided for taking Elaine's class intrigued me. This was evidently where the healing arts were headed. The fact that Elaine was accredited versus all the hocus-pocus healers I had crossed paths with made her special. I was thirty-three years old when I received the flyer and Elaine's name first was brought to my attention. It was placed in a folder, but the seed had been planted.

Thirty-four years of living my life, led from a place of fear and desperation, was taking its toll on me. Transition was happening, however the facts remained the same. I was damaged goods, wrung out from life and spiteful of those who had "sob-stories," like how they stubbed their toe or their mom was mean to them one day. I held onto the anger of my abuse and neglect because it drove me forward, it was spite in fact, I later found, that kept me alive.

By the eighth grade I was sixty pounds overweight and wore a 40 DD bra. Trust me, in 1980-1990 few people my age were heavy, the epidemic hadn't settled into our culture yet. I was pretty much an outcast. I hid behind the smile and people-pleas-

ing nature that helped me to fit-in, again, to a new school. Eighth grade was my sixth new school and by twelfth grade there would be eleven. By the third high school I attended, the use of alcohol and recreational drugs was the best tool I found to numb the pain - and manage friendships in my turbulent life. Friends were a place I could excel, there were so few. In denial of all institutional systems, especially schools and non-trustworthy adults, I retreated into more destructive patterns, the first of which was overeating, which began when I was an adolescent.

Interestingly, dreams began to surface of more extensive sexual abuse that I carried in my surface memory. As my earlier youth tumbled back into my consciousness, destructive patterns were deepened, anger, shame and the ridiculous facade I'd created, became who I was for ten more years.

Finally, fate drew me to a man who loved me despite of the wretched person I was inside. There had never been that experience, his love and my eventual home sanctuary became a large force of stability. Through practice, I began to trust. Before this point (in reflection) I had not been open to healing. I had not allowing myself to see the possibility to extend myself beyond the awfulness that I had experienced. I later learned that healing couldn't be achieved if it cannot be seen, until I could allow myself to consider the possibility of a better, whole life.

You see there had been jail experiences, numerous, dangerous, self-inflicted reckless times, and only a few good ones up to this point. Even if I thought of a better life, application was no closer than a dream... Then Elaine's flyer came into my life again.

It was a miraculous day when I noticed it was the same flyer as the one in my drawer! I got into contact with her. Amazingly, she was the most humble and gracious person I'd ever met. Elaine's eyes sparkled; she was just genuine and kind. No promises to change my life, no bells and whistles! She didn't even take credit for the ability she claimed to have, just that she was "Jumper-cables."

I soon understood what she meant when she said that the energy just flowed through her. Our session was as real as the nose on my face, the things I experienced were earth shattering and I was surprised that the whole time we were still in her little room, nothing physically had changed. I explained the experience to a few as clearly as I was able, "Like the Green Mile, when the big guy sucked the poison from Tom Hanks and the others, he blew out those bugs, I expected Elaine to do the same!"

I went to sleep that night, sleeping harder than in my whole life, awakening like everything inside had shifted and I was different. I wish I could say that it was a happy ending right there, but healing isn't always that clean and easy! I had created a lifetime of adjustment and accommodation for my pain, patterns which were still in place. The next few months would see a dramatic progression toward the REAL change, becoming who I am now... a completely different person.

I had modified my life to survive, was dependent on my anger and pain to feel a driving force, but now that was gone. I was not afraid to relax, not afraid to sit quietly and hear the still voice inside, the happy one I never got to know. No more being afraid that the pain would surface and sweep me away if I relaxed. Spending years and years in that state of fear and being on a path that was false and miss-led, that had been my life.

Now I am a full-time nursing student. Learning to learn in a school setting was the most difficult thing I have ever accomplished. I didn't mention that the previous educational experience held nothing but embarrassment and social opportunities; I started in college at the basics. Elaine even helped with that integration process, tying the previous pain to the accomplishments of my present, a sort of replacement I cannot explain.

When the foundation gets fixed, everything accommodates and straightens up too! With my current grades and plan for the future, HUGE help will be offered for children who have gone through experiences similar to mine. My past can now inspire my future, instead of direct it.

I now have control over the pain that used to control my life, and while still there, my past does not ruin my life. Without having met Elaine, there aren't enough horrific details I can conjure up to describe the potential dead-end I could have experienced. Thank you Elaine, from the bottom of my heart, soul and spirit."

N.L.

THE BEAUTIFUL RIBBONS OF LOVE

"Rest satisfied with doing well,
and leave others to talk of you as they please."

Pythagoras

Angel Message Received March 15, 2007 4:35pm:

"This evening, we ask that you open your hearts to new and won-
drous ideas. Thoughts that your mind may have only glimpsed
on occasion - now let them be ideas that are as fresh as spring-
time. Look through your precious eyes and see your life anew.

We, your Angelic and Spirit friends, are ever by your side, with
the heartfelt desire for you to loosen the reigns that fear and
anger had held on you. It is these reigns that can melt away from
you and be like beautiful ribbons that can decorate your life.

All trials, all difficulties, all situations and events that have oc-
curred throughout your lifetime have had one purpose and one
purpose only. To help you see who you truly are. Not the victim
of circumstances, although that often is the human view. Rather,
each moment gives you the opportunity to stand within Truth.
Truth is the blessed balm that soothes weariness and brings light
to bear on unfolding events.

Genuine Truth is not an emotion that erupts from a long held si-
lence, but Genuine Truth is the shining forth of goodness upon

148

yourself and others, allowing situations to change as you stand in your Powerful Strength of Truth and Love. It is not judge and jury, it is a place of quiet acceptance of the events of life that have brought you to this moment of understanding of who you are.

Too often, humankind has viewed Truth as the "facts" that justify an action. That is not truth but forceful opinion. Genuine Truth asks one thing and one thing only: Who do you wish to be in relation to someone or something?

It may be "true" in your experience, that someone has been unkind or unjust. But the Truth in that situation is that the Observer is watching fear in action. Fear is the Truth when unkindness is present. Fear is the Truth when others are angry. And the Truth of Fear is that Love is not Present.

So, in this time together, let Truth bring you to an understanding that Love is the most important ingredient in Life. Love of Kindness, Love of Justice, Love of Compassion, Love of Friendship, and Love of Life.

At all times, Stand in Truth and Goodness. If you are unsure of something, do not say you know what you do not. If you are confused, ask that you be given the time to find clarity. If someone is unkind to you, say at that moment, your words are bringing pain and uncertainty, how can we bring kindness here? Stand in Truth with Love in your Heart and invite the Joy of Truth to be your signature, and your life will change, starting now."

I had been invited to do a group reading at a young woman's home. She had gathered several of her friends together for the evening and when the time came for me to give her a message the Angels wanted me to ask her what her question was. "Do you think that we will ever be able to have a baby?" She shared that they felt a bit of pressure to conceive and immediately I saw the number two flash in front of my eyes. "I have a feeling that you will be having two babies, and sooner than you think." She said that she didn't know how that was possible because it seemed as though she and here husband were unable to conceive. "All I can say is that the Angels are showing me the numeral two, so that is what I have to say to you."

About a month later, I received a call from the hostess. "Elaine, you are not going to believe this! My husband and I just got a phone call telling us that there were twin girls in need of a home, and they asked us if we would be willing to adopt them. Our answer was an immediate yes. You were so right! We would be getting two babies at the same time, and we couldn't be happier!" They lovingly and joyfully shopped for enough supplies for two babies, and before they knew it, their family was complete. They had the children that they always wanted in their lives, and two little children were blessed with a loving home and two wonderful people who would share their lives with them.

THE ANGELS AND ME

TRANSFORMING SORROW INTO JOY

"Continue to express your dissent and your needs,
but remember to remain civilized,
for you will sorely miss civilization
if it is sacrificed in the turbulence of change."

Maximus of Ptahhotep, 3400 B.C.

I wish that I had always been diligent in recording the responses to messages that were given at each and every Audience Angel Reading, but in truth I don't recall every one. However, I do see how messages have corresponded to private readings that I have done, and this is an opportunity to share that insight with you. The following is the Angel's message yet the experiences that follow this message took place at another time, yet is pertinent to this message of how we allow our angers and thoughts about others to stop our growth and awareness.

Here is the Angels Message:
"What you give comes back to you. Whether it is kindness or anger, that which you give to another will be yours also. Before the utterance of words of anger, stop to see what you are bringing into your own life. An angry thought, an angry word and unkindness does far greater damage than you have ever realized.

There is a rippling throughout your hour, throughout your day, throughout your life, that will reach the shore of the end of your days and you will have to take time to view that which you have created. Has your life been like the gentle, rhythmic lapping of water on the shore, bringing comfort and inspiration, peace and friendship? Or will you look back upon your life and see injury in your wake. It is up to you to make that conscious choice. Do not create woundings that can shake the foundations of love that is needed in life. When anger is on your tongue, ask yourself, "Is this what I want in my life?" If not, speak your needs with kindness and power, not with willfulness and force.

In your interactions, have you brought understanding? In your thoughts, have you wished only for what is good? In your communication, have you brought forth peace in your presence?

Many are in the midst of contemplating the transformation of life into death and back to life again. In the traditions of Passover and Holy Week, reflect upon this message.

Life is the vehicle for your Soul to grow - yet it is not the only time of growth. When you leave your physical form, you will reflect upon your life, and those in it, and see who you have chosen to be. Transformation is your Soul's Journey, transforming sorrow into joy, anger into love, confusion into clarity, turmoil into peace.

In your life, be a Peace-bringer, a Peacemaker. Make Peace the mark that you leave upon the hearts of others. The woundings you give are the woundings you own. The love you extend is the love that carries others forth even as they encounter difficulty in life. Do not add to the discomfort by adding heaviness to the hearts of those in your life. Rather, bring Peace, bring Love, bring Kindness and gather all of your actions, words, thoughts and deeds as the blessings that your life brings forth through the remainder of your days."

As often happens, clients tell others about our experiences together and recommend that their friends come to see me. A woman came to have a private reading and, after explaining how things work I began as I usually do. I always state the date and ask the individual to state their full name. This does two things. It helps them to recall when the reading took place, and it puts their vibration into the dimension of sound. It is as if, when their voice is heard, those beings that wish to come forth can bring themselves closer to the individual, since our voices are distinct vibrations.

Immediately, in the left side of my field of vision, several feet back from my client, I felt the distinct presence of a male. I knew that this individual had two Angels with him, one on either side. His energy was peaceful yet sad. Often when the spirit of an individual has Angels immediately beside them it generally indicates one of two things…that the person had committed suicide or that they were in some kind of spiritual turmoil.

I asked my client if she had a brother, and angrily she said, "I am not talking about my brother, I am done with my brother, and I don't want anything to do with him!" Her tone was firm and I knew that she meant it. However, the Angels had other plans. "Well, whether or not you wish to talk about him is one thing, but the Angels are saying that they will be talking about him," I replied. Still visibly upset she said, "I did not come here to talk about my brother, I came here to talk about me. I have spent years talking about him and I have had enough. As far as I am concerned, I don't have a brother." Oh boy, this might be a challenge.

Quickly and quietly I asked the Angels what they wanted me to do, although in my heart I already knew. They wanted me to calmly convey their messages to her without being defensive or feeling attacked in any way. This was between her, her brother and the Angels, and truly, it had everything to do with the opening of her heart.

"There is no denying that your brother is here and that his life choices have not been the best. His actions have affected everyone, but it is time to let the anger go. It is time to change your point of view, because it has caused you too much bitterness, which in turn closes down your heart." I had asked if she knew where her brother was, and to her knowledge he was living on the streets somewhere. His lifestyle of drug and alcohol abuse had destroyed relationships, preventing him from being responsible in work and other family and social obligations.

The Angels wanted her to know that she had the right to be disappointed, but the anger was hurting her, and ultimately, her angry thoughts towards her brother were more powerful than she realized, being a detriment to both of them. I chose my words carefully and said, "What if you could just sit for a moment and think of your brother as a man who was full of fear. And, not wanting to admit his fear, he was willing to put himself in harm's way by taking drugs and other things. What if, rather than allowing anger to creep into your thoughts whenever your brother came to mind, you could simply send him love? Imagine him in your mind's eye as he was before he made the choices that he did. Imagine that you could see that he was full of fear, and that the only thing that could diminish his fear was Love. Would you be willing to try that?"

Reluctantly, she thought about her brother and, instead of being angry, sent him loving thoughts. It wasn't easy for her, but it was important. There was a shift from anger to a softer emotion, and she was able to see that her anger did not help anything, least of all him. Rather, anger can prevent us from looking at the possibility of change, even if it is just the way we think about another person or event. Imagine that you could see the situation as if you were looking at someone who was deeply wounded and was unable to see that Love could be in their hearts and in their lives, especially love for oneself.

Truly, the Angels have helped me to see, time and time again, that our judgments and willingness to hold onto our beliefs and angers can and will prevent miraculous changes from occurring. It is the simple yet profound change of heart that opens the doors for wondrous things to occur. When we relinquish our judgment and send loving thoughts instead of angry ones, we change the vibration of the memory, of the people involved and of our very souls.

We often neglect to comprehend that the quality of the way we think of one person can affect the way we see everyone. We see the world through the veil of our emotions and either mistrust others or enter each day with open and loving hearts. It is the quality of that vibration, the vibration of Love that is truly the Healing Balm that we are all in need of. In fact, it is the only healing power that exists.

At the conclusion of the reading, I had to tell her that from where he was standing and that I was seeing two Angels by his side, this could mean one of two things; either he was no longer in his physical body or, his spirit, while still in the physical world, was reaching out to her, beyond the physical limitations of space and time in order for his soul to continue to grow in the understanding of the purpose of his life.

He was being given an opportunity to mend a bridge, and, with the help of the Angels, walk to the other side once he told his sister of his love, desire for forgiveness and awareness that he had been given about the reason for living. That to give and receive forgiveness, even when we don't want to, is an act of Love - for ourselves and for every person in our lives.

Gentleness speaks louder than a blaring trumpet.

LOVE...THE ELIXIR OF LIFE

*"We don't get what we want.
We get what we are."*

Anonymous

Audience Angel Reading Message, June 4, 2007 - 12:38 pm:

"Let your Hearts be full... Full of Love, Full of Compassion, Full of Understanding, Full of Wonder.

Most of you walk through your life with a heart empty of love, but full of anger, confusion, or worse, resentment. Open your hearts to the magic of Love. Not the Love that brings you what you think you desire, but the Love that flows from you, endlessly, to others and to yourselves.

There is an endless source of Love, which is truly the Elixir of Life. You are here to experience and express Love in all of the thousands of ways that can be done. Most human beings do not understand the value of the Precious Gift of Love.

Love is the Energy that brings Life, brings Hope, brings Good-ness, brings Joy, brings Laughter... that truly brings Life.

You have all known people who walk through their life as the Walking Wounded, who do not allow the Essence of Love to bring them back to their senses. Literally, when you have your senses about you, you are able to perceive all that is around you. Most walk around numb, in a constant state of disbelief or disillusion. Change your heart and change your Life.

Give Love as the gift that it is. Love is never meant to be a tool of manipulation, although is it often used in that way. That is not love - that is lack. Love enfolds, love comforts, love gives an encouraging word, love smiles, love forgives, love lets go, love moves... constantly. Feel Love pour from your Heart into every moment of your life. Do not hold it back. Tell those that you Love how much you Love them, and tell them often. Send the blessing of Love in your thoughts to your day. Bring Love with you everywhere you go. Open your Hearts... You will be glad that you did!"

I was invited to the home of a family through a referral. I was given the directions and had never been in this area of the state. As I drove, for some reason I felt as though this was going to be an interesting night, and one that I would just have to trust what was going on and to say what came to mind, no matter how odd it seemed. There were five members of a family gathered together in the living room of their home. I felt a certain uneasiness and I wasn't' quite sure why. Everyone was very kind so I was not sure what to make of this feeling.

As I began, the young man to my left was the first one that I spoke to. "Has your Grandfather passed?" I asked. "Yes, he has." "He wants me to tell you that you have been seeing him. That he has been fiddling with the lights, and you thought it might be him because he was a bit of a handyman. Does this make sense to you?" With a shocked expression on his face he simply said "yes."

I began to hear someone swearing saying, "God damn it woman, tell them that I am here!" Well I have to say that I am not accustomed to having someone in spirit swear at me, but it didn't seem threatening in the least. It just didn't feel right to share it quite that way.

Next, I looked at one of the women and said, "Your father is making me feel like he is taking responsibility for his death. I am feeling heaviness in my chest and he is making me feel like he died of lung cancer. He is saying that his own actions lead to his illness. I smell smoke (but that seemed obvious, since they all smoked), and he wants to tell you all to quit smoking right now. He keeps saying, "Tell them to throw those God Damn cigarettes away!"

"That's Dad all right," one daughter said with a laugh, "that was his favorite expression." So I shared with them that he was talking to me in the same way he would have spoken, that way they would know it was him. He continued to use his same vocabulary, and they all laughed, knowing that it was their father.

His mood changed to a softer tone, and he asked me to say the following. "I wish that I had been kinder to all of you, that I would have listened to you and had been there for you. I want you all to know that I love you very much. Believe in yourselves and know that you can be anything that you want to be. I love you all." There were tears and laughter as they felt the burden of his heart begin to lift. He had been a tough man on the outside, but had a kind heart on the inside. His message for his grandson was especially poignant. "Believe in yourself, you can do great things if you just give it a try."

Friendship brings to life the reward of truth and compassion

BE GRATEFUL

*"Never regard study as a duty, but as the
enviable opportunity to learn to know the liberating
influence of beauty in the realm of the spirit
for your own personal joy
and to the profit of the community
to which your later work belongs."*

Albert Einstein

July 16, 2007, 4:11pm, Audience Angel Reading Message:

*"Dear Ones, You allow your hearts to dwell on the perception of
loss, rather than the creation of abundance. You already have
abundance. You are standing within the great well of the Energy
of Love and you do not know it. It is time for the connection to
be acknowledged, for the Source of Life to be your fuel that brings
all that you need to the fore.*

*It is the belief in disconnection that is the greatest human tragedy,
because it is truly an illusion. Just as you stand and breathe the
atmosphere around you, so too are you standing within the grid
of Life, the Grid of Love, and the direct current to All that Is.*

*The message this evening will be short and sweet. Feel Love. Be
Love. Act with Love. Bring Love everywhere...for truly that is
all there is.*

Do you say that you cannot love, or that you do not love? Which is the reality? Love yourself with kind regard, and you will love all that is around you. You will love the air you breathe, the food you consume, the fragrances you enjoy, the touch you feel, the words you speak, and the concepts you think. Bring your creative force of Love to all that you do with gratitude and a thankful heart. Be in the moment and experience the moment and you will soon realize that loving the moment brings preciousness to the moment.

One by one, these moments, embraced with love, will make up the totality of your lifetime. Live it, Love it, Embrace it…there is nothing else you need to do, except be Grateful.
Now open your hearts …"

There were two women in the audience that evening, Jill and Melissa, one that I had met once briefly through a friend, and the other I had never met before. As I was drawn to the side of the room where they were sitting I felt strongly that I needed to speak to Jill about animals. I later learned just how important the information that I shared was for them, and a precious four-legged wonder named Tillie. Much later, I would have the opportunity to meet Tillie in person, and it seemed as if she knew me immediately. The following is a confirmation of the information that I provided that night.

"What I remember about your angel reading relates to a reading you did for Jill. You didn't know her at the time, but had met her once. You asked if Jill was considering a new line of work, which she was considering heavily at the time. Then you asked, "Is this work with animals?" Indeed it was, as Jill was taking a course in providing physical therapy to animals and was considering opening a clinic. You stated that you were "seeing" two dogs. Jill said, "Yes, I have two dogs." You mentioned that you

were seeing two dogs that looked the same and had unusual coloring, like collies (which Australian Shepherds do resemble).

You then asked if one of the dogs was "different" or had a problem. Jill replied yes, one of them does, but she did not elaborate on the problem. You stated that you were "seeing" that something was wrong with an energetic connection in the dog's brain or neck. Jill replied that the female dog Tillie had recently been diagnosed with clustering epilepsy and that the vet believed the cause to be hereditary. You said, that you believed otherwise and said you were getting a signal that Tillie had a brain injury that was blocking (you used the term shorting out) the proper flow of energy to her brain. Jill and I were both amazed that you could "see" this, and were relieved to know that, while the illness was traumatic, it had not been caused by the breeder.

Since this reading, we have worked to find alternatives to treating her illness. We have used alternative medicine – chiropractic adjustment, moved from Phenobarbital to an old fashioned compound of Potassium Bromide and Valium (only after a seizure). All of this has helped. In fact, I believe it has saved Tillie's life. Tillie went from having six grand-mal seizures each month to within a twelve-hour period having ZERO seizures for one-and-a-half years. We thank you and the angels for directing us to help her."

Melissa

BRING GOODNESS TO WHERE YOU STAND

"A man, after he has brushed off
the dust and chips of his life,
will have left only the hard, clean question:
Was it good or was it evil?
Have I done well – or ill?"

John Steinbeck

Thursday, November 1, 2007 - 5:46 pm:

"Let us begin immediately by allowing you to have something to think about. Today, in the tradition of some, is the celebration of All Saints Day. This has been the day set aside to honor all those whose life events have been recognized and were considered to be saintly. This does not mean that these people were perfect or without fault, but rather, through the actions of their lives have been recognized as "good" or "pious." It is good to recognize the goodness within a human life, yet, we caution you in your notion of this distinction.

Each and every one of you should be celebrated this day, just as those who have been referred to as "saintly."

Each and every one of you should be celebrated this day and every day of your life. This day should serve to remind you that all peoples of the Earth, with no distinction of class, race, creed or belief are any less able to be "holy" in the most precious sense.

165

To be "Holy" does not mean that all of life must be restricted; or that which brings joy to life must be forfeited so that one might be seen as saintly. Rather, look to your own life, and bring goodness to where you stand. In every moment, you have a choice to be your best self. And, as you make that choice, be grateful to be aware of each and every precious moment of your life here on Earth.

Let this day be a reminder, not just on this day, but every day, that your Life has value beyond measure. You are more valuable than the greatest treasures in existence. Be not afraid of Holiness...it is your Souls' Natural State of Being."

Clients come into my life at interesting times; usually it is to help both of us understand life more deeply, and to allow us to stretch beyond our limits and comfort zones. Often, that is when the greatest awareness is given. The following is an email from a client who had contacted me as her mother was passing. She later confirmed how important that information had been so that her mother could
easily leave her worries behind as she left her physical form.

"Sometimes I feel as if I live for memories. As I let my mind wander back to a year ago I recall being with my mom as she was dying and I am flooded with wonderful memories. You see, Mom believed in Angels! As I sat with her during those final days I was able to give her support, but I also received support in return. One memory is particularly vivid to me.

For a few days, Mom had been speaking out loud to those who had already passed before her. What I did not realize was that those who had passed before her were visiting her in her room and supporting her also. I did not realize this until one particular visit occurred. My husband Bob and I were sitting in her room.

THE ANGELS AND ME

Mom asked, "Who is the little girl sitting in the chair?"

Neither of us could not see a little girl in the chair. Immediately Bob said, "Caitlin (our daughter) is in the kitchen eating dinner." A few minutes later Caitlin returned to Mom's room. "The little girl is here now," Bob said, thinking that Mom had been talking about Caitlin. But seeing Caitlin, Mom had a look of horror on her face; she seemed confused and frightened.

During the late hours of that evening Mom started to stir and began shouting out to those who had passed before her. When we came into the room Mom said, "I know who the little girl was. It was Margaret!" Margaret was my mom's daughter who had passed away as an infant. This experience has given me so much comfort in knowing that those who have passed before us will be there to love us and help us when we leave this life.

As it was obvious that Mom was getting close to dying. I contacted Elaine to find out what I should do to help her. She was struggling and I wasn't sure what to do. Elaine told me to tell my mom to look around for the Angels and her loved ones. She told me to tell her that she will have nothing to fear and will be embraced by their love.

Shortly after the our conversation, I went back into my mom's room and said, "Mom, I just spoke to the Angel Lady. Look for the Angels and those that you love and know that everything is okay. Look for the Light Mom, and you will be fine. I love you." Shortly after that conversation, with loved ones both living and passed standing by her side, Mom gently took her last breath. Thank you for your help."

Deb F.

Love must
be brought
to the other
as a gift · not
a reward

THE ANGELS AND ME

DIVINE + FORCE = AMAZING

*"You can preach a better sermon with your life
than with your lips."*

Oliver Goldsmith

Many of my experiences and lessons of working with Divine Beings happen when I least expect it. Often, when I am doing Energy Healings wonderful things occur that stop me in my tracks and cause me to be awed by the wonder of all that is taking place behind the scenes in life. Sometimes, things are almost too amazing to believe, but believe we must when all the elements lead us to a new understanding of who and what we are in this grand adventure called Life.

During each of our lives, intricate connections are being made long before we are ever aware of them. Call it Fate, call it Coincidence or call it Luck. It really doesn't matter. The only thing that matters is that we Pay Attention.

In October 2007, a woman came to me for the first time as a new client. Her name is Sheila. She was frightened, she was sick and she had just been diagnosed with pancreatic cancer. She nervously explained that she had been guided to me, guided in a way that she did not understand, but was willing to allow healing to occur. She explained that she had been trying for quite some time to learn what was wrong with her, but visit after visit to physicians gave no conclusive answers. She knew something was wrong, but did not want to alarm her family until she knew what it was.

Out of the blue one day Sheila received a call from one of her cousins who is an intuitive. Since she did not frequently speak with her cousin, Sheila's first thought was that something must be wrong, or God forbid, someone had died. "You are right, something is wrong," her cousin said, "someone is sick, and that someone is you." Sheila was stunned. What her cousin did not know was that at that very moment she was driving to have a CT scan to learn if she might have cancer. Her cousin told her that she needed to find and work with a healer immediately.

Sheila didn't know any healers, and so she asked someone that she thought might know one, her longtime friend, Bonnie. Interestingly, Bonnie did know someone...me.

Bonnie and I had first met as we sat next to one another in a class for hospice volunteers. Later, we were both hired by that same hospice organization, worked on the same team and became instant friends.

Shortly thereafter, Sheila and I began to work together. She was undergoing both chemo and radiation in preparation for a major surgical procedure called a Whipple procedure that was scheduled for January 2008. We worked together many times, helping her body prepare for the upcoming surgery and deal with the affects of both the chemo and radiation.

Sheila asked if I could be there for the surgery to do healing work before and after the procedure. I was happy to do so. Sheila's children came in from around the country and we sat together along with two of her dear friends. The surgery was a long one, and after ten hours of surgery, and two more post surgery, we were allowed to see Sheila.

Now, this is the interesting part. You see there was a wonderful young man who worked at the hospital who was the Patient Advocate. His honest to goodness name is Divine. Yep, that's right, his name is Divine.

Throughout the surgery, Divine would let us know how the surgery was progressing. Heidi, Sheila's daughter, asked when the two of us could go into the recovery area to see Sheila. She pleaded with Divine, telling him that the surgeon had given permission for me to be with her (which he had) in order to assist with her recovery.

Finally, Divine came over to us and said, "I can take you back to see her now." As we walked, Divine looked at me and said, "Why didn't you just say you were a healer, I could have gotten you back there much sooner." Good question, I thought.

As we walked into the recovery, Sheila was having some difficulty, as they had realized that her epidural was not working, and she had essentially no pain medication in her system and had just had major abdominal surgery. Her blood pressure was high and her blood oxygenation was low, all observable on the monitors.

As I began to do healing work with her, Sheila quietly said, "Elaine, you must be here because I can feel you." She slightly opened her eyes to see for herself. She often joked that she could "feel" my energy as I approached her home, and here in the hospital, half conscious, she still could feel me by her side. I was on the right side of the gurney and Heidi and Divine were on the left. Heidi said, "Oh my gosh, her blood pressure is stabilizing and her pulse ox is going up. This is very cool."

Just a moment later, the anesthesiologist came rushing into the room and stopped as he saw me. "You are doing healing work, aren't you?" he asked. "Yes, I am." He asked me if he was in my way, and I said, "Please, I don't want to be in your way."

He worked to get pain medicine into her system as I worked to ease her pain. He looked at me and said, "I wish I had a healer in every recovery room. I don't know exactly what you are doing, but I know that it works." I smiled.

I continued to work while he administered the medication. When he was done, he stood to the left of Divine on the opposite side of the gurney from me. Since I had noticed that his nametag was flipped backward, I could not see his name, so I asked, "Do you mind if I ask your name?" In a flash, he flipped his nametag over, and my body was full of tingles. "Force, my last name is Force."

As I stood in the recovery room looking at the two men across from me, I read their names, "Divine" and "Force," standing side by side. Divine Force was definitely in the room.

I am happy to say that Sheila is considered a survivor of pancreatic cancer, with no markers for cancer in her body. She always tells her friends and physicians about me, but I know that it is really Divine Force at work. I am grateful.

ELAINE M. GROHMAN

Let your heart be seen in your actions

A LITTLE PEANUT IN THE BIG APPLE

*"Goodwill is the one and only asset
that competition cannot undersell or destroy."*

Marshall Field

Those Angels can be rascals. Yep, that's right, I said rascals. Often they will steer you in one direction, and you are pretty sure you think you know what is going on, and before you know it, what you thought was going on isn't at all. Rascals!

The following was a message given to me to read to the group gathered for an Audience Angel Reading, but in truth, it was going to apply to me directly. Here is the message for the group reading on December 4, 2007, and by the end of that month I would be presented with a possibility that would be landing me, a little peanut, in the middle of the Big Apple.

"For many, your life is in the process of learning to Seek Spirit. This is a noble endeavor, but one that you do not completely comprehend. You often spend your precious time seeking rather than finding, striving rather than sitting still. You see, Our Dear Ones, within the precious space between moment to moment, that is where Spirit resides. The moments themselves are where We can be found. Look then with unseeking eyes, and we will reveal ourselves to your willing hearts.

So much human time is spent in thinking about the past, worrying about the future, rather than Being Here Now, it this precious

177

Moment of Time. It is to this silent space, this endless measure between your heartbeats that your attention must be drawn. Do not seek that which you perceive to be unattainable, but rather, know that you are Here Now in the Grace of Spirit. It is a concept that may appear foreign to you at this time, but once you allow yourself to reflect upon the comings and goings of your thoughts, you will begin to grasp this reality.

With lists upon lists you measure your time. Planning ahead or longing for the past prevents you from Living This Moment.

Set your lists down, sit your self down, and simply breathe. Breathe in the awareness of your quieting momentum. At first it will be uncomfortable to do so. Give yourself this gift anyway, no matter how reluctant your mind is to this seeming "waste of time." There is no wasting of time in the quiet moments. Unlike the hectic movement from one event to another, from one longing to another, when you stay in your Holy Quiet Space, we are able to be heard.

Bless yourselves this day. Bless yourselves this season. Bless those that you know and Love. Bless those whom you need to forgive. Bless those that have offended you. Bless yourself for having offended others. Release yourself from the untruth of believing that we are far from you. We are by your side, always and in every way.

Gift yourself with awareness of the Wonder of Spirit. We are Ever By Your Side, in your Heart and gratefully joining you on this Journey. Seek and you shall find, ask and it will be given to you. Your Joy is our Joy. Your Peace is our Peace. Your Love is the whole purpose."

The week of Christmas 2007, a friend came to see me. Pat grew up in Detroit but was living in New York City. I had met Pat several years before when my dear friend Kathy Mullen, a.k.a. Mully and I went to visit her childhood friend Karen, who was living in Manhattan. To make the trip worthwhile for me, since funds were tight, I offered to do Angel Readings while I was there. Karen magically arranged everything and before I knew it I had five readings to do while we were in New York. One of the people I did a reading for was Pat Jones.

Pat is an amazing woman... bright, articulate and fun. Each and every time I went to New York I would see Pat. So when she came home to Detroit to visit her family over the holiday she called to see if she and her sister could come over for a reading. I looked forward to seeing them.

When Pat arrived, she had barely taken her coat off when she said, "Lainie, I have been talking about you to some people for about six months." "Who are you talking to, and what are you talking about?" I inquired. You see Pat was working in the television industry, right in the heart of all the hustle and bustle of it all, Time Square. She told me that she had been talking with some producer friends about the Angel Readings that I do and thought that it might make an interesting pilot for a television show. "Would you be interested in something like that?" she asked. "Well, sure, that would be cool," I said, thinking quickly about all the things that could go wrong, like me getting cold feet and the Angels deciding that they were done with me. Nervous might be a good word to describe how I was feeling.

By the end of her visit, Pat promised to be in touch and before long, true to her word, she had arranged for me to meet three sets of producers. In February 2008 I boarded a plane for LaGuardia, giving myself an extra two days to be with another friend named Marianne who lives an hour outside the city. I knew that Marianne would be able to help me prepare for going into the city and my meetings with the producers. I didn't really know just how much I would need Marianne's help.

Marianne and I had met three years before in Salisbury, England at a Crop Circle and Stonehenge conference and became instant friends. Marianne is not only a brilliant computer program designer, she is also an extraordinary astrologer and student of Ecstatic Trance Postures, which I knew nothing about until that weekend. She had been a student of the astrologer/author Barbara Hand Clow, and had extensively studied the mysteries and the power of these postures. Soon I would understand, firsthand, just how much impact they could have.

I had arrived on a Friday and was scheduled to go into the city on Saturday night, do readings all day Sunday and meet the producers all day Monday before leaving Monday night to return to Michigan. Marianne and I enjoyed our time together on Friday and she was amazed at how accurately my astrological chart matched the events that were taking place that weekend. But Saturday morning I awoke with a terrible headache, which escalated into a migraine. I was in so much pain that I was nauseous, in short, I was a train wreck. We walked, we asked for assistance from nature, we sat on huge boulders, but I still felt terrible.

Marianne suggested that we consider doing an Ecstatic Trance Posture called the Bear Spirit Posture, which employed the medicine of the bear and the power that it holds to help a shaman in the transitions that they might encounter. "After all, you are going into the city, and you are giving them an opportunity to change their whole thinking about what a show could be. You are being their shaman, their healer." Marianne explained.

With Marianne leading the ceremony, we blessed the seven directions, East, West, North, South, Above, Below and Center, then she rattled a medicine rattle while we held our bodies in an ancient ritual posture and I received a healing that completely took my pain away. I was exhausted but no longer in pain.

Marianne drove me into the city and Pat and I spent time that evening talking about our mutual thoughts for a show. Sunday was full of readings and Monday we took the subway to Time Square. Wow, what sensory overload!

To her infinite credit, Pat never told me anything about the producers that I would be meeting, except their first names. She and I wanted everything that I might get for them to be fresh, with no preconceived notions about the people I would be meeting. It felt right.

The following morning as we made our way to Time Square I prayed that whatever was in the best interest of everyone would occur. Her office was in the Paramount Building, immediately across from the ABC studio. It was all very exciting.

The first two gentlemen that I met had an office close by. Walking into the lobby we were approached by a big Irishman named Tom. He had that Irish twinkle in his eye that is undeniable. As we walked into his Tom's partner Mike's office, Pat introduced me then asked, "If Elaine should happen to get any intuitive information for you both, can she share that with you?" "Yes," they both relied in unison.

I was asked to tell them a bit about myself, so I shared how I was introduced to Energy Medicine and then ultimately the Angels. As I spoke, I noticed that Tom's aura was glowing. I stopped and said, "Tom, I have to tell you that your aura is a beautiful violet color, and I am getting the impression that there is a maternal figure standing to your left. Has your mother passed?" "Yes, she has," he said, looking a bit surprised. Immediately his deceased mother wanted her son to know how very proud she was of him, and went on further to give me very specific information about him. He simply looked at me with tears rolling down his cheeks. Then, I noticed an elderly gentleman with a cap on his head, sitting some distance back, on the radiator actually, and he had a mischievous look on his face.

Then I heard the unmistakable Irish brogue. My own grandmother had come from Ireland and an Irish brogue was something that I recognized immediately. "Tom, was your grandfather on your dad's side from Ireland? Because I am hearing a man say, "Tommy, me boy, tis been the longest thyme since I had seen ya. How are ya lad?" "That is my grandpa, and that is exactly how he sounded," Tom said with a huge smile on his face. I tried my best to replicate his brogue, recalling how my own grandmother sounded.

Then I looked over towards Mike and I felt an overwhelming sadness. What a drastic difference in just a moment's time. As I looked at him I heard and felt a female on the maternal side, his left, but I somehow knew that it was not his mother. "Mike, there is a woman standing next to you and she is making me feel like she died of cancer in this area (as I placed my hands on my lower abdomen). This is someone who is a maternal figure, but definitely not your mother. Do you know who this might be?" Mike looked at me with a stunned expression and said, "Yes, I know who it is. It is my wife."

She continued by saying, "I am so glad that you did not give up on love, because my death was so hard. Thank you for all the loving care that you gave to me. I am so glad that you are happy now and that you did not give up on love." Immediately I heard,

"Tell him I left behind a three-year-old." So I repeated those words exactly. "Does this make sense to you?" I asked.

With tears welling up in his eyes he said, "Yes, my wife died when our son was just about to turn four years old." She went on to tell me that she did not want to die but that her body could no longer survive the ravages of cancer. She wanted him to know how much she loved him and she wanted her son to know that she did not abandon him, and that she loved him very much too. She continued and wanted me to share that she was responsible for Mike meeting his second wife, and that she was so happy that he was happy. He told me that he had always felt that she had something to do with him meeting his current wife.

Within a matter of a few minutes, Mike held his hand up and said, "You don't have to say another thing, I know you are the real deal." The two men then enthusiastically talked about the ideas that they had about how they might be able to create a show, and how we might be able to help others see their lives differently.

As the meeting concluded, Pat and I walked out into the hallway and stopped. "Do you realize that we were in there for one and a half hours, and that the typical meeting with producers it about twenty minutes, tops. That was really amazing." We hugged one another and I thanked God and the Angels for their constant help in communicating with others about important information. And that was only the first of three production companies I was scheduled to meet that day. As the second producer came to Pat's office, she was clearly distracted and somewhat disinterested in the whole concept. I later learned that Pat knew that this would be the case but wanted me to have an experience of different types of producers and their personalities.

The last set of producers was a wonderful husband and wife team.

They came to Pat's office with their beautiful baby daughter, Lily Gabriella. As we sat at the large table both Maddie and Pedro had their backs to the large picture window facing Time Square. As with the others, I gave them a bit of information about myself and then asked if it was okay if I gave them any intuitive information if I received any.

The moment they said yes, I immediately looked at Pedro and said, "There is a man here who says that he is your father, and it feels as though he is deceased." Pedro quietly nodded in agreement. "Your father wants you to know that he is very proud of you, and that you are a better man than he ever was. He is asking if you could forgive him, he wishes that he had been a better father. I am also feeling that you had your own Divine encounter in which your life was saved. Did you have an experience in which there was gunfire and you were in the wrong place at the wrong time? I am feeling like Archangel Michael protected you that day. Pedro, it was not your time to die, and you were completely surrounded by his energy. Does this sound right to you?" Pedro sat dumbfounded.

I then brought my attention to his wife, Maddie. As I looked at her sweet face she said to me, "Elaine, I have heard the Angels speak to me my whole life, and this morning, they kept saying to me, "You have to meet this woman, you have to meet this woman." I thanked her and began to relay the information that I was receiving for her. She nodded her agreement, confirming the information that I was sharing. As we talked I couldn't help but be memorized by the image that was on the screen across the street in Time Square, directly behind Maddie in my view of her.

The magnificent statue called "The Angel of the Waters," the centerpiece of the Bethesda Fountain in Central Park, was projected on the screen across the street. From my point of view, it appeared as if the wings sprouted out of Maddie's back, as she sat quietly in front of me. "Maddie, you are an angel in the life of many people, especially your dear husband, Pedro."

As I sat in stunned amazement, I asked Pat, who was sitting to my left, if she could see the wings too. "Oh, I see it, it's beautiful." With that, I knew that something extraordinary had occurred that day and I was so grateful as I took a cab to the airport. It had been yet one more example of the presence of Angels in our lives, and the wonderful ways that we can bring messages of love and understanding to one another, if we care to pay attention. I later received the following email from Pedro regarding our conversation that day.

"I've been thinking about you since the day we met and I'm very glad to have met you. I walked away from our meeting with a sense of relief. Perhaps, because in you I saw someone whose belief is impenetrable by the negative... Or perhaps, because my father (my weakness) is proud of me and I've never heard those words before. Thank you.

Angels, I believe in them. I believe they have brought me and Maddie a permanent smile to share with the world in our baby girl, Lily Gabriella. At a time in my life when the want or need to smile was but a distant emotion... I believe Angels have saved me more than once and I believe they are by my side as I walk through this journey within God's shadow...

Elaine you have a gift and the fact that you want to share your gift with the world without taking away integrity, dignity or someone's self respect leaves me extremely optimistic. A show that can benefit not only the believer but the one who is lost..."

We did go on to shoot a pilot with one of the production compa-

185

nies and, unfortunately it was not picked up by any network, but, I feel that the real reason for my visit to New York was to give messages to the people I was fortunate enough to meet. Who knows what will happen... someday?

Look people in the eyes
when you speak to them —
that is where heart
meets heart.

THE MEDICINE WALK

"To be what we are,
and to become what we are capable of becoming,
is the only end of life."

Baruch Spinoza

Sometimes we are given opportunities to be the spokesperson for God. We don't always know it and we may never know the impact of the words that we share and how others are affected by those words. It is an amazing experience when we are pressed into service, at a moments notice, and we just have to learn to go with the flow, and Trust what we are saying when it seems to "come out of nowhere."

Native American healers have a special knowing that many of us have lost. They have a term, "Good Medicine," which has nothing to do with medicine at all. "Good Medicine" is anything that helps someone, whether that is a smile or a kind act. "Good Medicine" can change a life, and can help one to know that they are greater than they have dared to dream. Kindness can heal unlike any medicine we know of.

The following is an Angelic Message that I received which would later serve to help me more fully understand that Trust can be one of our greatest gifts.

"As you walk this Earth, pause for a moment and think about the direction that you wish to travel. Not only in the actual movement

188

from place to place, but in the movement from moment to moment, from thought to thought, from breath to breath. As you go forward, from this moment on, begin to consider the journey that you are taking. Do you hastily rush though your day, through your week, through your life, in the illusion that you must get somewhere? Were you to consider that each moment IS the journey, would you plot your travels with more care?

We wish for you to remember that you walk the grounds that have been traveled by generations before you. The lineage of humanity that have blessed or brought harm to this Earth are your ancestors. Are your steps forward taken with a sense of adventure or with worry, anger or with joy? Do your thoughts linger in the times gone by, endlessly tumbling your discontent over in your mind, giving strength to your identity as an injured soul, one who had been wronged, one who is angry? Or do you recount those moments that have brought pearls of wisdom to you, brought wonder to your mind, peace to your home and a smile to your face?

Each step that you take in this lifetime is a step towards the ultimate understanding of the reason for your birth. When will you choose to know that reason, live that reason, and bless that reason, and every experience that has brought you to this moment? This is, after all, the only moment that you have, This Precious Now. No longer spend your breath dwelling on your past, but rather bless each sorrow, each joy, and each event that has been a gift of self-understanding, even when confusion or sorrow brought you to your knees.

Who are you now because of those past moments? Are you wiser for them, are you more compassionate for them, are you more loving for them? And, as you look to your future, do you allow that longing to obscure this Precious Moment, do you endlessly grasp what is beyond your reach, beyond your knowing, perhaps even beyond your future steps?

Rather, look around you at this moment, and see the gifts that are offered to you right here, right now, as you sit within your own Holy Space, the space that is You - Your Energy, Your Vitality, Your Being. In this moment, are you a gift to those who are by your side? As you go from this evening, is the memory of you re-called as a gift?

It is only when you are aware of this Precious Moment in Time, this very moment, that you can heal who you have been and be the person that you Truly are. As you become aware of this Gift of Present Awareness you stand within the Holy Moment of the Now, in which you can relinquish all that you have carried thus far, and Invite Love, the True Gift of this Life, into your Present Moment, Now.

This will change you, it is truly the only thing that can, and it be-gins inside of You. Be Present in your Life and you will be a gift to everyone that you encounter. Do not forget how important you are. As if you could understand that you are a cell in the Body of God. Be a healthy one, full of Love, Peace and Compassion. Heal this Earth with each step forward, with deliberate intent to bring Love to each Moment of this Sacred Path called Your Life."

I had been invited to be a guest on a talk radio show. As I was explaining to the host the work that I do in both Energy Healing and Angel Readings, he asked if I would be willing to do spon-taneous on-air readings…like, right now. "Ah… sure, I could do that," I said as he quickly flipped to a commercial break. Please Angels, I am going to need your help here. I had never done a call in reading before. I had to put my trust in my Divine Friends, and as always, they didn't let me down.

As I was being re-introduced the host told me that there was a caller on the line who wanted to know anything that I could tell her. Immediately I asked if there was someone who had recently passed, a young man in fact. "Why yes, there is a young man, my niece's boyfriend." I immediately felt that he had died very swiftly, in a car accident, and he wanted his family to know that he had not suffered. She confirmed that he had died in a car accident. Yet, there was something very important that he wanted me to say.

"Is there a baby?" I asked. "Yes, my niece is pregnant," was her stunned reply. The young man wanted so much to get a message to her. "Please tell her for him that he loves her very much and that he did not wish to die and leave her alone. He wants his family to help her, to be supportive to her, so that his child will know that he loved this baby, even though he will never be able to hold his child." Before I knew it, the host said that it was time to take a break, and would I be willing to talk to someone else. "Wow!" was all I could say.

After the commercial break a young woman was on the line. I asked her if she was in nursing school. "No," she replied. I kept hearing "Caregiver, caregiver, caregiver." And then I felt that someone had something wrong with his or her eyes. So I asked, "Are you a caregiver? And does someone have difficulty with their eyes?" "As a matter of fact yes, I just started a job today as a caregiver for an elderly woman and she is blind." Then I heard, "World War II," so I asked if World War II made any sense to her. "No, not really." Then I saw someone writing in a book, similar to a journal. "Are you sure that there is nothing to do with World War II? I am also seeing a journal."

I then heard a slight gasp. "Oh my goodness, I just learned today that my client was a survivor of a concentration camp." "That's

191

it," I said, "please do both of you a favor. Ask her to tell you her stories. It will be a tremendous gift to her, since she has had a very heavy heart, wondering why she survived and so many others perished. She had felt guilt about this for years. Please let her tell you her stories... write them down for her. She helped so many with her kindness and she needs to know how important her life has been. And, your life will be greatly enriched by hearing her stories...she lived history. Will you do that please?" "Yes, I will, thank you," said the young caller quietly. Then, in a moment, it was on to another commercial break.

The following day I received an email that took my breath away. The woman who had been a caller into the show the night before emailed to let me know that the brief reading stunned her. She said that she could hardly think after she hung up the phone. She wanted me to know that the young man who had died in the accident had not even been buried yet! His funeral was the following day. She had just learned of his death shortly before her call, and she was so grateful to be able to know that his love was strong enough to get through to his family, even if it was through a woman on a radio show who was listening to the Angels between commercial breaks. Thanks guys!

I am always so grateful for their unending love and support, even in the most unusual circumstances. If one trusts... then there is nothing to worry about. The Big Guns have it covered!

THE ANGELS AND ME

THE VOICE OF YOUR HOLY SELVES

"Humility is the solid foundation
of all the virtues."

Confucius

Angel Message – Friday, April 25, 2008 - 12:03 pm:

"This day, know that you are blessed. This day, know that you are loved. This day, know that your life holds more promise, more joy, more wonder than you have ever allowed yourselves to consider. Now is the time to consider this, indeed it is time to Embrace It.

This wondrous time that is upon you now is the Gift that you have been longing for. It is not something extraordinary, yet it is Extraordinary in its Ordinary Nature. It is the gift of this moment, of this Sacred Now, it is the gift of your Life, right here and right now. This is where you begin, this is where you end, this is where you explore and create, this is the gift that Awareness brings to you. Now and Forever. It is not out there, it is within your Sacred Self.

This evening, just relax. Let go of all of your notions that you hold dear. They are illusions that invade your moments and distort your awareness of who you are. It is this time, this precious moment, in which you can begin to Breathe in the Breath of Life… knowingly, with peace in your Heart and Wonder in your Eyes, and Love in your Being.

Listen to the gentle voice that is awakening in you… the voice of Love, the voice of Peace, the voice of Forgiveness…the voice of your Holy Selves. We, your Friends, offer this peace to you, not as a gift, but as your birthright. It is yours to embrace, to bring into your own Hearts and then, with loving awareness, share that peace with those who walk this life with you. Together you will change the Hearts of Mankind and Heal your precious World. You have that Power within you…Use It Well."

I had been scheduled to give two talks at a Women's Expo, one on Energy Medicine and the other an Audience Angel Reading. Each were scheduled and advertised as fifty-minute talks, where normally I would have two hours for an Audience Reading.

The Audience Angel Reading had close to one hundred people in attendance. When I began, I simply asked the Angels to guide me to whoever was in need of their message, and, since this was such a large group of people, I knew that I would not be able to speak to everyone.

Funny thing about those Angels, they have a mysterious way of directing people to sit in a particular area of the room, and, more often than not, people who sit in an area together often have the same concerns, or even more amazingly, the messages given to one seem to apply to more than one person. Clever rascals!

I was drawn to a beautiful woman who had the look of both sadness and bewilderment on her face. I started with her. There was a message from her deceased mother, offering comfort and strength. I truly do not recall all that I said to her, and in short order it was time to move on to someone else.

As I approached another woman, I felt a father figure standing next to her. He showed me a scar on his face, just under his right eye and encompassing part of his cheek. Then I heard, "shrap-nel…" loud and clear. Indicating to her where I felt that there was a scar on his right cheek, under his eye, I asked her if this made sense to her as it related to her father. "Well, he was hit with shrapnel when he was in the war, and, he had a scar on his face in that exact spot." With that information being acknowl-edged, he asked me to convey his thoughts to her. "Your father seems very humbled by this opportunity to give you a message. He wants me to convey to you that he is very sorry that he was not the kind of father that he hoped he would be. He wants you to know, first and foremost, that he loves you very much."

"He is saying that he was a very young man, perhaps late teens or early twenties when he went into the military and that the shock of what he saw changed him forever. At that time, no one knew what Post Traumatic Stress Disorder was, but he knows now that he suffered from this. After coming home from the war, he went from killing people and seeing much destruction to being treated as a hero, expected to pick up where he left off, and he feels, that he did not do too well at that." He went on to say that he had a difficult time expressing his emotions, and before he knew it he was married with children and the responsibility of taking care of his family. He was distant with his children and he wanted his daughter to know how sorry he was that he had difficulty expressing his love but he wanted her to know it now.

Before long, I was on to another person, asking her to begin to take better care of herself, knowing that just because there had been a history of disease in her family did not mean that she had to be another victim. She could consciously take better care of herself, and thereby live a long and happy life with her son. Be-fore I knew it the fifty minutes were up. I thanked everyone, in-cluding the Angels, for being there to assist in this communication.

196

One never knows how intricately the lace of life is woven to bring us together in the sands of time. About a week later I received the following email.

"By some force I came to one of your talks at the Women's Expo for Mind, Body & Spirit in Birmingham. I had planned to spend both days at the library working on a difficult project. I wandered across the street to check out the Expo and never made it back to the library. I had also picked up a copy of the Metro Times, which I rarely read, and saw the ad for the Expo the day before. My point is, something was steering me to you.

After your message from Archangel Gabriel on forgiveness, it became my theme that day and I have been working with it ever since... you entered the audience and started with me. You zeroed in on important issues and also brought my mother to light. It was important for me to hear from her for the second time in as many days. I was shocked at the time, because I did not know what you do. I am new to the whole thing and had never before been interested in 'hearing' from loved ones. I say this also believing we are all one and pick our parents and who we are. You also mentioned that I would make a good healer.

This is why I'm writing. I recalled someone telling me at that Expo that I should have my chakras cleared, mainly my heart chakra. My husband of thirty-one years left me in October and I have been working on most levels to heal from this. I am thinking chakra clearing could not hurt! So, I have been wondering for days if you do that. I have also been looking at your website and noticed your Sacred Geometry class. Imagine my shock upon hearing you on the radio today talking about just that. Another sign?

I worked a bit on myself this week (before I heard your show) and one time had amazing results, but I don't know if I can tell if I'm cleared. I also saw your light as you wandered the Expo...so I think I have some aptitude. Yes, like the man in Europe, I also think you are the 'real deal.'

My question is this... I have an interest and inclination to take your class, and I would also like your counsel. What can I expect if I take the class? Is 'Sacred Geometry' energy healing? I listened to your show as you explained your practice and was able to clearly understand what you were saying. I look forward to hearing from you"
Marianne

One never knows how our words will be used to assist others in their own personal journey, but it is my prayer every day... that I be an instrument of Peace.

*Set an example
by your words
& Deeds*

THE IMPACT OF A TRANSGRESSION

*"Let us not look back in anger
or forward in fear,
but around in awareness."*

James Thurber

It's time that we take a new, more responsible look at our actions, or lack of actions. It is time for us to take responsibility for everything that we do. We can no longer afford to say, "It's not my fault," or "I am this way because of this or that person, or this or that event?" We need to stop!

We no longer have the luxury of turning away from situations that are destructive and imagine that we shouldn't get involved or that it is not our problem. Every transgression is our problem. There is no other way to make a change for the better without taking responsibility for what we are aware of. We have to take steps to help our children understand that they are capable of changing events by changing their thinking and thus changing their actions.

Keep in mind that children become adults, and if we fail to help our children learn how to cope, we will find ourselves with adults who are unable to cope. We cannot afford to fail to teach these lessons. We must help our children know that they have the tools to bring kindness and strength into their lives.

The following is from the Audience Angel Reading on Thursday, June 26, 2008 - 4:36 pm:

"Know that every action or lack of action has an effect. Whether that is a transgression that happened long ago or something that happened moments ago, acts that do not bring Love forth need forgiveness and recognition. Recognize when people have not been handled with care. Recognize when the need to be right has had more weight at the moment than the need to be kind. Kindness should not be confused with weakness. Rather, let kindness be brought to a situation by no argument at all. Simply drop the need to be "right" and allow another to have their say. Often, it is the need to be heard that is what is being called for. Listen with an open heart, and there will be more understanding.

Many make the error of judgment. The false need to defend oneself in the midst of a heated discussion, or in the midst of a power play of one form or another, builds walls between human beings. Rather than defend, take a breath and ask, how can goodness and kindness be served?

The growth of the Spirit as it travels through lifehoods in the recognition of the totality of its Soul, is the ultimate goal of the experiences in Life. When one interacts with another, or refuses to do so, there is a balance or an imbalance that takes place.

This does not imply that one should not take action when a situation is not tolerable. But yet, in a moment, you may be given the opportunity to recognize whether the "intolerableness" of a situation may be your unwillingness to change or forgive. No amount of time can change the impact of a transgression; indeed it may increase the depth of emotional injury. The act that changes a transgression is forgiveness. So when you are called upon to bring kindness to a situation, do so without hesitation."

THE SUREST GUIDE

"Enthusiasm is self-confidence in action."

Franklin Field

The constant in all of the Angels' communications is Love. First and foremost, Love for oneself. This is not in any way a selfish act, but rather a wise thing to do because in truth, if we loved ourselves, we would never harm another in thought, word or deed. It would be incomprehensible to us, knowing that we are truly all connected, and what harms one harms us all.

The Message from the Audience Angel Reading Message - October 30, 2008 -5:33 pm:

"Speak softly, speak surely, and speak lovingly. Know the importance of your words. Be certain and know that your words have value and that your words should be heard. All too often, we see you hold back. You hold back when things should be claimed, when things need clarification, and when Love needs to be made present.

We ask you, in this time, to speak from your Heart. Your Heart is the surest guide. Your Heart will help to filter the anger from your thoughts. Your Heart will bring pause to the moment, and within the silent breaths that you take, bring your Heart clearly into your communications.

With the changing times that you are experiencing now, and the changing times to come, know always, that change has ever been the hallmark of humanity. Change is necessary and change is good, if that change calls you to be your most Loving Self.

If that change enfolds all of Humanity within its outstretched arms then a thunderous change will ripple though the Heart of Humanity so that you may finally truly see that you are all One.

The One that has presented all of life at your feet merely asks that you recognize that you are not the only recipient of the riches of the Earth. Each and every Soul has been given these gifts from the Creator of All that Is, just as a loving mother brings food to all of her children.

Open your Eyes and open your Hearts to the needs of all of Humanity, and it is then that wars will cease, hunger will be no more, and Humanity will finally see who they are through one another's eyes. You are the gift for the whole Human Race, each and every one of you. You are the protector of the Land, You are the keeper of its riches, You are the guardians of all Children and you are the Light that we have all been waiting for. Let your Light shine so that each one may know who they are…together as One."

There is never a time that the Angels have given anything but encouraging, loving and hopeful messages, both for myself and for others. So many times we feel that our own words have little value, or that they will not be heard at all by those to whom we need to speak. Yet often our words, when conveyed with love and acceptance of others will open doors that we thought would never be presented to us. The following is from a young woman, who, after a private reading had the courage, when the time was right, to say what she needed to say to one of her siblings, and thankfully, it helped her to know that her words were important, and heard.

"After I left your house, I felt very weird. I had this new ultra-awareness about myself. Everything you told me, sort of made my world make sense and gave me a confidence about what I was thinking in my head, but wasn't saying. Something specific you told me, actually just happened. I am the youngest sibling, and rarely in the role of telling people what to do. But, you told me I needed to speak to my older brother about his diet and to start exercising. I thought, "yeah right, he'll never take me seriously." But, about two years after I saw you, he initiated the conversation, and to my surprise he listened to me and followed through with everything!"

Following her heart, when the time was right the opportunity presented itself. She opened her heart and spoke her concerns, and to her surprise, the information was not only received but fully taken in. I love it when that happens!

TELL DADDY FOR ME

"Tears, idle tears, I know not what they mean,
Tears from the depth of some divine despair
Rise in the heart, and gather to the eyes.
In looking on the happy autumn fields,
and thinking of the days that are no more."

Lord Alfred Tennyson

For some reason, as yet unknown to me, there was urgency to the message that was to be relayed that evening. As usual, I was prompted to sit to write, and within a few minutes the message was recorded. As I read the message, I felt a slight tug to my heart.

The Angels Message from December 11, 2008 - 2:45 pm:

"Time passes quickly. In the blink of an eye a day is over, a week is over, a month is over, a year is over, and a lifetime is over.

It is the blessed gift of time that we would like for you to pay closer attention to. Moments of precious wonder surround you at all times, yet so often those precious moments are missed by a racing mind and your furious pace of life.

Take a moment, now in this quiet space of togetherness, and breathe in the essence of Time. Breathe in this moment and begin to feel the space of time that is needed to breathe, to breathe in

207

and to breathe out. Just this conscious connection to your breath can slow you down and allow for you to become aware of where you are in the Here and Now.

Take Time this day, in this hour, in this moment, to realize that your Life here on this Planet is a culmination of eons of time. Never before this moment could you have been here before this present instant. Every step that you have taken has brought you here - right here, right now. It is that awareness the can cause you to pause, and capture the enormity of this Time, this precious now. It is your Time, Treasure it and use it well."

Immediately upon sharing this message, I was drawn to one young woman, as if I was pulled to her like a magnet. She told me that her name was Beth. Without hesitation I began to relay the Angels message, "The Angels want you to know that they hear your prayers, that you pray all of the time." She quietly nodded her agreement. "They want me to say to you that you pray constantly, and that you are praying for two people, children in fact." "Yes," she said, "I am constantly praying for two children."

Then an image came into my mind. I saw a little girl in my mind's eye, and she was securely holding a teddy bear with her right arm, clutching it close to her body. When I see these images, I know that I have to share the message of the visual. So I said, " I am seeing a little girl, perhaps three or four years old, and she is clutching a teddy bear (and at this point I demonstrated what I was saying by holding my right arm as if I was holding a bear). Does this make any sense to you?"

"Yes, it does. That is the way that we buried our little girl, with her teddy bear in her arm, just like she used to walk around with it." My heart felt both sad and joyful in a most unusual way, one that only the Angels seem to make me feel. She told me that her daughter's name was Phoebe. Phoebe then said to me, "Tell Daddy it's not his fault, tell Daddy it's not his fault, tell Daddy it's not his fault." I repeated her words exactly, then after hesitating a moment because I could feel the intensity of her need to be understood, I asked her mother if that made sense to her. Again, with tear filled eyes she said, "Yes, it makes sense. You see, our daughter drowned, and my husband was there when it happened. I was not there at the time." Everyone at the Audience Reading was in tears, hearing the pleading of this precious little girl.

Oh, my heart felt so much pain for her, but strangely, at the same time Phoebe wanted me to let her mother know that she was fine. Then she showed me what happened. "She was having so much fun and in her excitement, she did not understand the difference between the surface of the ground and the surface of the water. All she knew was that she saw kids in the pool having fun, and she wanted to join them, so she started to run. In her innocence and exuberance she just started to run and when she hit the water she was laughing and took in a full breath of water, completely filling her lungs. She is saying again to tell her Daddy that it is not his fault."

It seems that her Daddy had his back to her for just a moment when she started to run. When he turned around she was already in the water, and it was too late. Then she showed me what looked like a white garment around her neck. It seemed strange to me, but I knew that I had to say it anyway. She was not sure what it meant. Later, we would find out.

Phoebe continued with more messages of love for her family and wanted to reassure them that there were Angels there immediately by her side, that she did not have any pain, and that she would always be with them. Then, she started to tell me of the other little girl.

So I asked, "Is there another child that you are praying for?" "Yes, one of my best friends just had a baby girl on December 1st. She had aspirated her merconium (fecal material) into her lungs and her little body was completely septic. They did not think that she would make it through the night the day she was born, and she has been in the neo-natal ICU ever since."

Immediately the Angels wanted me to have Beth tell the baby's parents what they could do to energetically assist in her recovery. She needed energy so that her body could begin to fight the bacterial infection that was ravaging her little body. Before long the reading was over and every person got a message. I was so moved by all that I had been able to share.

The following day I received a phone call from Phoebe's mother asking if she and her husband could come in for a private reading.

the loving thought of a friend
is an angel of God
sent
to carry a benediction to the soul.

stead

THE OPENED DOOR

"Nothing is impossible;
there are ways that lead to everything,
and if we have sufficient will,
we should always have sufficient means.
It is often merely for an excuse
that we say things are impossible."

Francois de La Rochefoucauld

The following Friday, Phoebe's parents, Beth and Matt, came to see me. Before they arrived I kept hearing two names, "Brandon, Brendan. Brandon, Brendan." Over and over I would hear those two names in my mind. "Brandon, Brendan." I knew that there was a reason that I was hearing it, and soon I would know why those names were important for me to remember.

Timidly, Phoebe's parents sat in my healing room and I explained to Phoebe's father how this happens for me. I thanked them both for coming and then I asked them if the name Brandon or Brendan made any sense to them. They looked at one another with a shocked look on their faces. "Brandon is the name of the boy who pulled Phoebe out of the water." Amazing, I thought, this is one strong little spirit, this little Phoebe. She wanted her parents to keep in touch with him since he was greatly affected by Phoebe's drowning and she wanted him to know that there was nothing he could have done. She also wanted to be sure that her father kept in touch with him so that the trauma of that day would not be an affliction to him.

213

Phoebe made her presence known without hesitation. She wanted to make sure that her Daddy knew how much she loved him and wanted to be sure to have her parents give her love to her siblings. In fact, she wanted them to know that her sister had seen her after her death but she was afraid to tell her parents. She wanted them to know that she was around them often.

This time, she showed herself in greater detail so that I could describe her physically. "I am seeing a little girl with beautiful blond ringlets, like nice soft curls, is this what Phoebe looks like?" "Yes," was their reply. Then she showed me a small pink barrette, on the right side, pulling her hair away from her face. She seemed to love this pink barrette. They told me that Phoebe often wore a pink barrette in her hair and that pink had recently become her favorite color. They did not need any further convincing that this was indeed their precious daughter.

Then Beth shared that she understood what I had spoken about the evening of the reading regarding some type of white fabric. "I had forgotten about it, but we placed her white blanket around her neck just before we closed the casket. This is how Phoebe would go to sleep every night, with her white blanket tucked under her chin. You were right about what you saw. I just couldn't think that night. It wasn't until I told my husband about it that he knew exactly what you meant." I am always so grateful when information is given and they are able to piece together the information that I shared with them.

Then a strange thing happened, Phoebe wanted me to say, "Tell them about the ten people, about the ten people that they know." So I asked if they had any idea what she might be referring to. She was letting me know that her parents were with ten people and after a moment they both seemed to understand what I was talking about. "We meet with a group of parents who have also lost their children. There are ten of us that meet once a week to try to help each other with our grief." As soon as they recognized who Phoebe was referring to, I started to receive information about the other children, how they died and the impact that their deaths had on their parents.

It was as if Phoebe held open the door and made it possible for the other children to give me messages for their parents. One by one, the children began to show me how they died, as if to help Phoebes' parent know which child was communicating with me so that they could pass the messages along to the other grieving parents. Two young men in particular stand out in my memory, both died in two separate car accidents.

I saw in my mind's eye as a young man showed me how he had been thrown from a car. I later learned that the vehicle he was a passenger in was struck by another car as the driver swerved to avoid hitting an object in the road. He wanted his parents to know that the Angels held him in their arms so that he did not feel the impact of hitting the guardrail. He showed me the exact size and location of the laceration on his head, but he assured me that he did not experience any pain at the time of his death. The Angels prevented him from feeling the impact. He wanted them to know that he was fine and that he loved them very much. I learned that this young man's mother had cried daily, thinking of the pain that her child must have experienced. He wanted to let her know that there was no pain. The Angels prevented him from feeling anything but comfort and love.

Another young man told me that he was drunk driving and he wanted his parents to know that he took full responsibility for his actions. It was nobody else's fault. This young man wanted his dad to know that he "shouldn't be pissed off at him anymore." I later learned that the father was comforted by this information, saying that this is exactly the way his son would have spoken. There were some parents that helped one another, as Phoebe's parents were doing, and then there were some that had little coping skills, turning instead to alcohol, or dealing with anger and experiencing deep depression. These children were hopeful that their parents would see things as they did, knowing that they were all right, that they loved them, and to take care of one another.

It was an amazing day and one that I will not soon forget. I am always so grateful to be able to share messages that bring comfort to those who are left behind, and to help others to know that there is so much more than what we can perceive with our human eyes.

I later received an email from Beth that brought tears to my eyes and goose bumps to my flesh.

"I did want to share something with you. In our session at your home, you asked if the name Sheila meant anything to us. We said "no" and then you mentioned it is like Sheila but possibly "Shylia." This meant nothing at the time so we moved on. That was on December 19th.

However on February 15th, another family joined our grief group. Their daughter had also drowned, but in the bathtub of their home. I felt this overwhelming anxiety and a need to ask immediately... "What was her name?" They said, "Shylia." I almost fell off of my chair. I knew it was going to be that as soon as they started to talk about her. I could feel it. She drowned on January 19th in their home and she was eleven months old. I wonder if Phoebe was there, watching her or waiting for her. It was so bizarre."

FRANCESCA - THE MIRACLE BABY

"Love seeketh not itself to please,
Nor for itself hath any care,
But for another gives its ease,
And builds a Heaven in Hell's despair."

William Blake

The December 11, 2008 Audience Angel Reading in which the precious Phoebe brought messages of love and support for her family, also brought information about another precious child, a miracle baby really, by the name of Francesca. During that Audience Angel Reading, I had been drawn to Beth, the mother of Phoebe, and the Angels wanted her to know that they had heard her constant prayers. From the loving heart of a mother who had lost her beloved daughter, she had asked that God and the Angels protect both Phoebe and Francesca, the infant daughter of one of her dearest friends. Francesca was not expected to live, and was laying quietly in the neonatal intensive care at Children's Hospital.

Francesca was born early in December 2008. Her mother, Maureen, was a first time mom and had concerns about her pregnancy. She had a nagging feeling that something was wrong, but time after time, and ultrasound after ultrasound, she was told that her fears were just that... fears, and that she had nothing to be concerned about. Her baby was fine.

She was scheduled for yet another ultrasound, and as she laid on the table the technician said with alarm in her voice, "There is something wrong." The medical team delivered Francesca and gave her parents, Maureen and Ronny, the sad news. It seems that Francesca had aspirated her merconium (fecal material) into her lungs, and she was not expected to survive the day. Her body was septic, and the poisons in her system were causing her body to shut down. Her lungs, kidneys, and other vital organs were failing. Little did they know that Francesca, whose name means "free," had a stronger will then they could fathom.

It was at the December 11th Audience Angel Reading, after re-laying their message from Phoebe to her mother, that the Angels directed my attention to the "other child" she was praying for. I saw, in my mind's eye, a frail little body, but at the same time, felt the strength of her spirit. The Angels wanted me to tell Phoebe's mother, Beth, what she could tell her friends to do for their baby to help her recover. I was "shown" that her energy was unable to move properly through her body, and I gave very specific instructions to Beth, asking that she share this informa-tion with Francesca's parents. The Angels wanted them to bring energy from her feet to her crown so that her little body would begin to feel energy once again.

Within a day or so, I received a call from Maureen, Francesca's mother. She asked if I would be willing to come to see their baby in the neonatal ICU. I readily agreed. Since her parents, grand-parents, and other family members were with her around the clock, I was told that any time would be fine. We made arrange-ments for me to go to see their daughter.

After meeting Maureen and her husband Ronny in the family waiting room, we walked together to the ICU to see Francesca. We scrubbed in and went to see their baby. As I approached her little swollen body, all I could see were tubes and monitors every-where. She lay perfectly still, and I was told that this was how she was all of the time. I asked her anxious parents to stand next to me so that they could watch what I was doing. I wanted them to know what they could do to help her regain her strength.

I placed the middle finger (fire finger) of my right hand on the very top of her head at her crown chakra, and my fire finger of my left hand on the bottom of her left foot. The moment I touched the arch of her foot, her big toe began to move. We all stood in amazement as her body responded to the Energy Healing treatment. I continued to work on her, explaining what I was doing and why. I instructed them to do what I had shown them each day, several times a day. Her parents stood next to me with tears in their eyes as the watched the monitors indicate that her vital signs were stabilizing, and that the healing was helping.

The nurses watched with interest and I told them that I was a healer, and that I was doing an Energy Healing on Francesca. I feel strongly that it is part of my responsibility to help those around me understand what it is that I am doing, and why. The more one understands something, the less likely they are to dis-miss it. I suggested to Maureen and Ronny that they play sooth-ing music for her, so that she could listen to sounds other than the whirl of the machines that surrounded her.

I later received a call from Maureen telling me that Francesca began to make improvements after her first treatment and that she and her husband would continue to work on her. But she still had a long road ahead of her. They asked if I would come back and we set a date. The next time I went to see Francesca, she had less tubes connected to her and she was more responsive. Her parents had a tiny I-pod by her side so that she could continuously listen to peaceful music. The last and final time that I went to see

Francesca, she had finally been weaned from the respirator, and as I approached her bassinette she turned her head to look my way. I can't tell you how that made my heart smile with gratitude for this precious little miracle baby. She seemed to recognize me and even smiled as I spoke her name.

After nearly two months in the hospital, Francesca was finally able to go home with her Mommy and Daddy. She is thriving and catching up with her baby milestones. Just the other day, I received an email from Maureen telling me some wonderful news.

Here is a portion of that message.

"Francesca is doing wonderfully. On Thanksgiving 2009, after the Thanksgiving Day parade, Children's Hospital is doing a special on three success stories, and Francesca is going to be one of the children featured."

What a blessing to have been able to witness the strength of a little spirit, coupled with the love of her family and friends that helped this precious little girl fight for her life. It will be a remarkable one, I am sure.

TOUCHING THE WEB OF LIFE

"I myself do nothing.
The Holy Spirit accomplishes all through me."

William Blake

I used to be surprised by things that happen. I am not sure that I would use that adjective any longer. In truth, I am constantly amazed and grateful. I can not deny that there are forces that intricately weaves events, circumstances, and seeming "by chance" happenings; all are guided by Divine and loving hands. There are no accidents, there are no mistakes, and those people who are directed into your life are there for a reason. We are blessings to one another, if only we would look through the eyes of Love to see the blessing. We so quickly misinterpret what we are meant to understand about circumstances and events by habitually falling into our own patterns of thought.

For one lovely woman, that pattern is taking responsibility for things beyond her control. When that happens, we inevitably walk away disillusioned, hurt, saddened, confused and all too often, exhausted. We wonder why things are as they are and why people do as they do. But if you were to step back for a moment and step out of your habitual patterning, perhaps then you might find a pearl of wisdom that has been hidden inside its shell. Allow me to explain.

A woman by the name of Karen happened to take a refresher nursing course at Madonna University. And it just so happened that class was being taught by my dear sister, Therese, a fabulous nurse and a beloved instructor. Therese is an extraordinary combination of humor, intellect, integrity, fun, depth and compassion. She teaches her students about the Heart of Medicine, not just the technicalities. They leave her care knowing how to care for themselves as they care for their patients.

At some point, Therese gave Karen my name, and Karen came to me for an Energy Healing session. Karen and I hit it off right away. From my perspective, I felt an instant kinship and comfort with her and I could see in her eyes the depth of her compassionate heart. Karen had a deep longing to be of service to others, yet, she wasn't sure that it was nursing that was calling her name.

We met for the first time on May 14, 2009. She had some confusion about returning to the workplace as a nurse, but the most pressing problem was her health. She shared that she was scheduled to have surgery to remove her parathyroid. The parathyroid is made of four glands of the endocrine system, whose function is to control calcium levels in the body. If it is not functioning properly, it can adversely affect the nervous, muscular and skeletal systems. She wanted to know if there was something that could be done to help her body help itself.

I explained what an Energy Healing could do for the body with the understanding that the body has a built in system of self-healing, if only there is enough energy to run that function. I often receive "intuitive information" while I am working, so I asked her if I could share any information with her that I might receive. She immediately said "Yes."

We worked together several times. Each time I would balance her entire body's energy and then concentrate on the parathyroid area of her neck. Her body responded beautifully to the Energy

Healing and she would leave feeling more relaxed, with less pain, and a brighter outlook. She had been scheduled for surgery but was concerned about the procedure. Then one day, I received an email from Karen that took my breath away.

"Hi Elaine, My internist called me on Saturday. He was very confused; he did not have record that I had the parathyroid surgery and just received my recent three-month blood work results. My calcium was normal, my parathyroid hormone was normal and my cholesterol dropped 30 points. I told him I had not had the surgery and was seeing a healer. He paused and said, "We don't ask questions, we are just grateful." I know I will have more dialogue with him next time I seem him. Thanks for EVERYTHING!"

The next time I saw her she literally glowed. Her weigh had dropped as her parathyroid function stabilized, and her energy level was higher than it had been. She looked great.

Then one day, during another healing, she received a beautiful gift of understanding how closely aligned our family can be to us, whether that person is alive or deceased. Love is the connection that ties soul to soul. Perhaps it is best to allow Karen's own words to speak to her experience.

"Dear Elaine, Thank you for today's session. You opened a portal that has been closed for the past six weeks, leaving me fatigued, overwhelmed, anxious, and confused. I am breathing again, filled with love and connection to my spirit. You use your gifts with compassion and care and I am blessed to know the grace that is you. Each session that we have shared has provided me with a deeper understanding of love. Through your healing energy, I have been able to acknowledge the presence of my guides, angels, and loved ones that have passed. I have seen their

eyes and forms, and have felt their hands working alongside of yours.

Today I experienced the featherlike weight of two small feet standing on my chest, just below my heart, with the vision of a giant wingspan above me. I felt the deepest feeling of love and acceptance possible. You have given me the precious gift of knowing that I am never alone, I am always loved, I am always cared for, and always given exactly what I needed. You remind me to be present to everyone I meet, will meet, or should meet, and to always listen for and hear the divine messages.

From one of our sessions - July 7, 2009:

You had a clear sense that one of my strongest guides was with us. You described him as man of short stature, but large presence. He was wearing a small black cap and a black suit in which the jacket was long, he looked very scholarly, possibly a religious man, possibly a rabbi or teacher. He had a mustache and beard, slightly graying and had kind eyes. He was standing with two other men. One man looked angry and bitter and had a large strawberry shaped mark on his face, possibly a birthmark, the other man had his arm around the bearded man and was smiling and laughing with him.

They were gathered looking at a tombstone, and the bearded man read the words: "Ben Shmuel, Menachim ben Shmuel..." and the man with the birthmark got angrier and angrier as the other two kept laughing. This is when you asked me "What am I saying?" Through my laughter and tears, I told you that you just spoke to me in Hebrew, "Son of Samuel, Max, the son of Samuel." And you continued with, "I have never spoken Hebrew before, I am a red-headed Irish girl."

I explained that this must be my grandfather, Samuel who died when I was very young, and the only pictures I had ever seen of him were as an old man. The other two men were his sons; one was my father Max who died almost to this day in July of 2005, the man who nurtured and raised me with unconditional love, devotion, and humor. The other man was his brother, the oldest and last surviving son, and he has a port wine birthmark on his face. In the Jewish tradition, the headstone is placed one year after the person dies at a ceremony called an unveiling, where family and friends gather graveside to remember.

At my father's unveiling, my uncle read the headstone and became very angry and kept repeating that we had spelled his father's name incorrectly in Hebrew, saying "It was not Shmuel, it was not Shmuel," and created such discourse. For the past four years, my mother had held on to this day and how this sacred moment was overshadowed by bitterness and anger.

When I shared my session with my sister and mother, knowing that our father, her Max, was laughing with his father, she was unburdened. We laughed and we were all in gratitude for the enormity of your gifts.

Weeks later, I was at my aunt's home helping her with some legal papers. She carefully unlocked a small metal box, gently lifted the lid, and there on top was a picture of her father, my grandfather, exactly as you had described him. With love, Karen"

Each session has been a combination of wonder, tears, relief and understanding. We would talk about the need to look at the circumstances that she observed in medicine and in life, not to take on the burden of not understanding what is broken with the system, but rather to look at the dysfunction to see what it is. You cannot change what you do not observe.

226

Often, our discontent clouds our ability to look at solutions for the problems. And sometimes the best thing that we can do is to gain the insight needed, and then walk away, so that you can bring the solution from the outside in. It is often difficult if not impossible to change a system when you are stuck in the muck and mire.

What I have been blessed to learn about Karen, and truly all of my clients, family and friends, is that at the heart of it all, we truly do want goodness and love in our lives, but we can't find it outside ourselves, it is within us. When we recognize that it is within us then and only then can we bring it out into the world. How cool is that to know that we have always held the solutions to the problems that surround us, if we only look inside our own hearts. Then we will not be willing to compromise care of another or ourselves ever again.

ELAINE M. GROHMAN

UNTIL YOU KNOW

*"Presumption can strangle the heart
and never allow true Sight to see what is so."*

Elaine M. Grohman

Audience Angel Reading Message

"Until you know, beyond any doubt, why people do as they do, do not judge. Until you know, the inner recesses of another's heart, do not judge. Until you know, the wounds that others carry, do not judge.

Instead, see within others the possibility of change. See within yourself, the choices that you have made in every moment. See within yourself, that judgment affects both you and the other, locking yourselves in a stance that minimizes the possibility for the unfolding of a new path, a new direction, and a new choice.

In this time of Spring, rebirth is literally just under the surface. You might bemoan the cold days, yet this change in weather does not negate the unfolding of the life that is yet unseen under the surface of the Land.

So too, do humans have the opportunity to allow themselves to blossom, when they are surrounded by a fertile landscape which provides the nurturance of acceptance, the water that allows old wounds to wash away and the sunlight of Love to radiate upon

228

another so that they can stand strong in the dawning of a new view of their life and be the beautiful Being they were created to be.

Until you know, give Love as the encouraging energy to allow a heart and soul to blossom with renewed Life."

On this particular day, there was a small group of women gathered for an Audience Angel Reading and I immediately was drawn to one woman after sharing this message. "I believe that this message is for you in particular, but certainly it applies to all of us, me included." She began to get a little teary eyed as she shook her head yes in acknowledgement. Her brother had just passed away, and clearly there were unresolved issues that troubled her. We did not press on - the message had been given and received.

One of our greatest challenges in life is to "know that we do not know." We do not know all of the reasons behind someone's actions or the events that occur in our lives. Too often we make presumptions that block understanding and therefore healing to occur. Sometimes healing is nothing more than changing one's point of view, to see something with fresh eyes, rather than to see people and events through the veil of our own wounds.

Many times people mistakenly believe that others intentionally do things to hurt us or to make us unhappy. We often forget that we are sometimes the "other" who may also be perceived in the same fashion. It is in our best interest to begin to let those presumptions go so that we can begin to witness what is under the surface of a situation. People only attempt to hurt others when they themselves are hurting. So, with that awareness in your mind consider what would happen if you merely stopped, quietly gathered your thoughts and energy and asked the other, "How does this help you to have this belief?"

During this same gathering, a beautiful older woman sat quietly in her chair. I was drawn to her and noticed that there were two male spirits standing by her side. As I began to tell her about them, she knew exactly who they were - they had been her husbands. They both expressed their love for her and one of them even acknowledged that he had been instrumental in bringing husband number two into his wife's life.

They both had loved her and were very grateful that she had been in both of their lives, and wanted to be sure that she knew that. They shared information that helped her to understand that it was indeed them, including acknowledging a beautiful aquamarine that one had given to her as a gift. They wanted her to live her life fully, and that they both looked forward to seeing her again.

THE NAIL

"Try not to become a man of success,
but rather to become a man of value."

Albert Einstein

A woman came to see me for an individual reading and as I always do, I explained to her what might occur. Since every reading is different, and I must trust that what I am being given is of some significance, I explain that I try not to "filter" what I am hearing, seeing, feeling or knowing, keeping in mind that what I say may not make any sense to me, but may make perfect sense to that individual. Yet interestingly, sometimes the information is obscure to the client and it is not until others hear the message that the information is comprehensible. Trust, integrity and an open heart are the key ingredients to any reading.

I always record a reading for the individual, asking that they not spend time writing, which can distract them from simply listening to the messages. I let them know that often something may not make sense to them at the moment but it may make sense to them at a later time. Many times I have received emails or calls from clients days, weeks, months or even years after the reading, sharing with me that something I had said finally made sense and that the event had indeed occurred.

I explain that it is often beneficial to listen to the recording every now and then so that they might have clarity about the information.

As I sat with my client there was a gentleman standing next to her on the paternal side. I asked her if her father was deceased, and with tears in her eyes she said, "Yes, I was hoping he would be here." Almost immediately I saw his hand as he held up a single nail between his thumb and index finger. "Was your father a carpenter or a builder? I am seeing him holding up a single nail, like a carpenter's woodworking nail. Does this make sense to you?"

She look puzzled and began to chuckle, saying, "No, my father never built anything, he was not really a handy man." Hmm, I knew that I was seeing a single nail, but since it did not make any sense to her, I did not press on in that direction. Many messages of love and support were given to her as we continued the reading and before I knew it the hour was up. She thanked me for the information and went on her way.

The next day I received an email from my client and she stated that she understood what the nail meant. After the reading she went to see her mother and sister and invited them to listen to the tape. As soon as they heard about the nail, her mother and sister looked at each other with a knowing look. They knew what the nail was all about!

My client's father had passed away very unexpectedly of a massive heart attack. He died with his overcoat on, and when they gave his belongings to his wife and daughter (my client's sister) there was a nail among his things. They had found a single nail in his pocket, a carpenter's nail, one that he had received from his church during Lent, to remind the parishioners of the Crucifixion, to remind them of another "carpenter." He apparently wanted to give a message to his entire family, wife and daughters and used the unexpected "nail" to bring them all together to listen to the message and be aware of his presence and love for them all.

Words—
once uttered from our
lips can
never be returned.
Choose your words with
care & love.
for the heart that
looks beyond the
moment
will know that love
in years to come.

CLOSE THE DOOR OF ANGER

"You can't turn back the clock.
But you can wind it up again."

Bonnie Prudden

"Let that which you think you comprehend be set aside, and open your hearts to Love that is real and is good. Do not think of death as a punishment, for it is not. It is a change, a transition of life from one plane to another, but let us assure you that Life goes on.

It is hard for the human mind to comprehend death, especially when it seems unfair or unjust. Life is and Life will always be the greatest gift that you can imagine.

Close the doors of anger today and let your hearts know that the continuation of Life is the journey that every soul will take. It is the journey to understand the totality of your Soul. And from the human perspective it looks like trial and difficulty, but from the eyes that see the total, it is the opportunity that you finally understand that each and every moment is a lifetime of experiences that are meant to open your Heart to Love. Love each minute, through the good times and the bad, and the sorrow that you carry today will be a gift beyond measure when you understand its purpose in times to come."

Since I have many clients that come to me to have private readings, rather than coming to an Audience Reading, I would like to

234

share a message that I had received from a client, who, as you will see, was not sure that an Angel could or would be able to give a message to her.

"Hi Elaine,

I went to get an angel reading this past January with my mom, who has long been a firm believer in angels and the spiritual world. While I do consider myself open-minded to this kind of thing, I have to admit that I went into it a bit guarded, as I just wasn't sure a woman I had never met before, through the angels, would be able to tell me anything meaningful and relevant about my life. I couldn't have been more wrong.

At the time of the reading, I had been trying to get pregnant for over a year without any luck, which was frustrating enough on its own. To top it off, I had just found out a month earlier that my younger sister was expecting her first baby in July. Needless to say, the whole ordeal had left me stressed out, depressed, and had done quite a number on my self-esteem. I mentioned nothing about this when I sat down for the reading, but you, through the Angels, picked up on it immediately. You asked me if I had lost a child, and when I said that I hadn't, you asked me if I had been trying to get pregnant.

You explained though the Angels that the reason I hadn't gotten pregnant yet was because I hadn't been ready. Around the time of my 30th birthday (a little over a year before the reading), you explained that I had started to love myself, and until that happened, I wasn't ready to truly love a child. You said that I would definitely have a child of my own, sooner than I thought, and that this child would be special and would require the kind of love that, until recently, I wouldn't have been able to give.

The messages of the angels moved me to tears. Any doubts I had

235

coming into this were completely erased by the end of the reading. How could you not be a believer when your deepest, innermost thoughts and feelings are brought to light? This wasn't a matter of guessing around until something was even the tiniest bit relevant. The reading brought forth very specific details of my life, which I believe could not have happened unless angels were truly involved.

The reading gave me hope, which is something that had been virtually lost to me up until that point. It made me realize that everything truly does happen for a reason, and even though I hadn't gotten pregnant yet, it was definitely in the cards for me, when the time is right. I left the reading feeling extremely content and peaceful, which at that point in my life, was a priceless gift."

Jan

THE ANGELS AND ME

EXPECT A MIRACLE

*"If we did all the things we are capable of doing,
we would literally astound ourselves."*

Thomas Edison

Message from the Angels - February 26, 2009:

*"This is it... this is the moment that you have been waiting for...
the moment in which you have thought that your life could and
would change. This is it, right here and right now.*

*It is in this magical moment, right here at this Present time, that
you can change your life by changing your perspective about life.
It is not you being here physically in this room, or physically sitting in your chair, but it is the Present Moment that you have,
each and every second of each and every hour, of each and every
day, that you have the opportunity to change everything about
your life.... all with your thoughts and heart.*

*For centuries upon centuries we have watched the human condi-
tion, as the moments of life are lost in time due to the thief that
resides within you. And the thief that robs you of the joy your
days should hold are those thoughts that keep resentment, judgment and anger at the center of your awareness and allow them
to grow stronger with every precious second you give it.*

*If for one instant you could overt your attention, and see that the
things that you choose to focus on only have the power over you*

that you allow them to have.

Tonight, in this precious moment of Now, please consider giving your self a gift. Allow resentment to loosen and release its grip on your heart, on your thoughts... truly, on your life. Resist the temptation to judge others, since in truth you can never know the full scope of the situation that you assume you comprehend. The chambers of the human heart, and the corridors of the human mind, are far too delicate and broad for you to comprehend as someone looking in from the outside. Truly, all that matters is that you begin to know that you do not know, and when you know that you do not fully know, you will not find the need to judge yourself or others.

Circumstances occur in life that are like pearls of wisdom in disguise. And those pearls often disguise themselves as seemingly difficult people or situation, things that might cause you stress, if you allow it to do so.

Give yourself the greatest gift that you can give yourself this day. Give yourself the gift of non-judgment, non-resentment, non-anger... give yourself the gift of Peace.

And one by one, the resentments, concerns and stressors of life can lose their hold upon you, and you will truly know that all is well, that everything is always in perfect order, if you will only trust that it is so.

This does not release you from the responsibility of acting with kindness and clarity. Do not stand by and watch negativity grow, but rather, stop it in its tracks, take away the wind from its sails, and it can no longer have the strength to direct the flow of your life. Allow your heart, instead, to guide the way."

Through the
waves of
Time

ACKNOWLEDGMENTS

From Me to You

It is hard to find the words to thank all of the people who have helped me in the process of writing this book. I must take this time to thank two people, Marala Scott and Tre Parker, co-authors of "In Our House – Perception vs. Reality" of Seraph Books, for their belief in this book and their willingness to help me bring it to fruition. I should have known that the Angels would always have a hand in this project.

When I learned of the name of their publishing company, Seraph Books, I could not help but recognize that "Seraph" is the prefix of "Seraphim," the highest-ranking Angels in the Choir of Angels, with Archangel Michael as their lead. Thank you for your commitment, your kindness, your friendship and your faith in me. It has touched my heart deeply.

With special thanks to all of the following people for your support and sponsorship. Marala Scott and Tre Parker, Alyssa Curry, Aaron Curry, Lainie Rubio, Robert Jarski, Ph.D., Dianne L. Haas, Ph.D., R.N., Carmen Siman, Leonard D. Wright, M.D., Jennifer Skiff, Jeffrey Zaslow, Chris and Jack Berry, Andrew Heyman, M.D., Marianne Carroll, Sara Warber, M.D., Judy and Bill Petrere, Mary Ellen Wojie, Jill Greenfield, The Jamison Family, Kevin and Kathleen Anderson, Ken Brenner, Brian and Isabelle Ribando, Rhonda Brooks, Robert Piepenburg, Rebecca Rosen, Georgina Walker, Mary Lou Zieve, Claire Bernacki, Nancy L. Skurka and Samantha Walasek.

241

And to all the many people who have allowed me to step into their lives, if only for a brief time, and to share what I am privileged to share with them. It is my sincerest hope that those who read this book will be changed - that they will look at themselves and others with kinder, more compassionate eyes, and know that soon enough our own lives will have been lived and will come to their conclusion.

We never know when or how this will happen, but it most certainly will. So, let's begin today to bring Love into our own lives and into the lives of those we love, work and share this Earth with.

Please know, that I will continue to work throughout my life to help to bring awareness to our precious planet and to those I am privileged to encounter, in whatever way that may be. Even if our only encounter is through the pages of this book, I will be grateful for that opportunity.

Please pass goodness along, it is charged with the Energy of Love. That is were we must begin.

With love and gratitude,

Elaine

REFERENCES

Rosalyn L. Bruyere
www.rosalynlbruyere.com

Marianne Carroll – Ecstatic Trance Postures
YourBodyKnows@optonline.net

Circles of Wisdom - Sharing the Teachings of Mother Earth
www.circlesofwisdom.wordpress.com

Barbara Hand Clow
www.handclow2012.com

Cuyamungue Institute
www.cuyamungueinstitute.com

Focal Point Photography
www.fpstudio.net
Farmington, Michigan

Elaine M. Grohman's artwork is available at
www.elainegrohman.com

John Two Hawks
www.johntwohawks.com

Healing Touch Center - Farmington Hills, Michigan
www.healingtouchcenter.info

Healing Touch International
www.healingtouchinternational.org

Elaine is wearing earrings by Jennifer Stephenson McLamb,
available at www.JenniferMcLamb.com.

Dr. Judith Orloff
www.drjudithorloff.com

Polarity Therapy Association
www.polaritytherapy.org

Rebecca Rosen
www.rebeccarosen.com
Denver, Colorado

Doreen Virtue, Ph.D.
www.angeltherapy.org

Georgina Walker
www.georginawalker.com
Australia

Jeffrey Zaslow
www.thelastlecture.com

ABOUT THE AUTHOR

Elaine M. Grohman is a Certified Healing Touch Practitioner, an Associate Polarity Practitioner, an Angel Therapy Practitioner, and the developer and teacher of an energy healing modality called Sacred Geometry and Energy Medicine – Healing from the Fourth Dimension. She has an active private practice in which she sees clients for both Energy Healing and Angel Readings. As an Angel Reader, she conducts Audience Angel Readings in which she gives messages of love and comfort to as many people as possible.

Along with her private practice, Elaine is involved with the University of Michigan Medical School's Integrative Medicine Program. She enjoys working with medical students, residents, Integrative Medicine Fellows, physicians, and medical faculty to help them understand Energy Medicine, Integrative Medicine and its place in health care. She also works with medical students from Wayne State University Medical School in Detroit, Michigan and their HuMed program for first year medical students. She is a guest lecturer at Madonna University in Livonia, Michigan in both their nursing and hospice programs.

She is the former host of "Going Beyond Medicine," on Psychic Radio, owned and operated by CBS. In that capacity, she interviewed experts, authors and individuals who are making a difference in health care through Integrative Medicine. Her guests also included individuals whose expertise helps to support self growth, health and awareness of Body, Mind and Spirit.

Elaine and her husband Rich live in Farmington Hills, Michigan. She is the mother of two wonderful human beings, Elaine Rubio and Brian Grohman. Her family is blessed with their son-in-law, Marvin, and their soon to be daughter-in-law Ronya, along with two beautiful grandchildren, Maria and Conner. Elaine is also blessed to have fifteen siblings, two of whom are deceased, many in-laws and a whole host of nieces and nephews. As you might imagine, there is never a dull moment.

Elaine teaches workshops and is available to speak to groups interested in understanding Energy Medicine, the Angels or other inspirational topics.

Elaine M. Grohman, CHTP, APP, ATP
Farmington Hills, Michigan 48334
248-855-3456
Email: egrohman@twmi.rr.com
Website: www.elainegrohman.com